Collins COBUILD

CONCORDANCE SAMPLERS
3: REPORTING

Geoff Thompson

THE UNIVERSITY OF BIRMINGHAM

COLLINS COBUILD

HarperCollins*Publishers*

HarperCollins Publishers
77-85 Fulham Palace Road
London W6 8JB

COBUILD is a trademark of William Collins Sons & Co Ltd

© HarperCollins Publishers Ltd 1995

First published 1995

10 9 8 7 6 5 4 3 2 1

The photocopying of material in this book is permitted within an institution, where multiple copies may be distributed to students for class use only. Otherwise, all rights are reserved, and no part of this book may be reproduced, stored in a retrieval system, or transmitted in any form or by any means, without the prior permission in writing of the Publisher.

ISBN 0 00 370938 8

Corpus Acknowledgements

We would like to acknowledge the assistance of the many hundreds of individuals and companies who have kindly given permission for copyright material to be used in The Bank of English. The written sources include many national and regional newspapers in Britain and overseas; magazine and periodical publishers; and book publishers in Britain, the United States, and Australia. Extensive spoken data has been provided by radio and television broadcasting companies; research workers at many universities and other institutions; and numerous individual contributors. We are grateful to them all.

Printed and bound by Scotprint Ltd, Musselburgh, Scotland

Contents

Introduction	4
Exercises	5
Guide to the Concordance Pages	10
The Concordances	14

said	14	demand	40
say	16	describe, call, define, refer	41
told	17	emphasise	42
tell	19	explain	43
asked	20	give, deliver, issue, make, offer	44
ask, asking	22	go, have it, run	45
thought	23	insist	46
think	25	is, as, was, were, been	47
according to, apparently, allegedly, to quote, in the words of	26	it	48
		laugh, gasp, groan, moan, sigh, sob	49
add, begin, continue, go on, interupt, mention	27	order	50
admit	28	order, promise, proposal, request, suggestion	51
advice, announcement, assurance, claim, comment, information	29	persuade, convince, dissuade	52
		point out	53
advise	30	promise	54
answer, reply	31	prove, demonstrate, show	55
apologise, nag, quarrel, scold, tell off	32	put it	56
as	33	remind	57
bark, growl, grunt, roar, snarl, snort, whine	34	shout, cry, exclaim, mutter, scream, whisper, yell	58
be	35	so, not	59
believe	36	suggest	60
claim	37	threaten	61
congratulate, bless, compliment, praise	38	warn	62
criticize, blame, charge, condemn	39	wish	63

Answers to Exercises	64

Introduction

Since the launch of the COBUILD project, there have been many requests from learners and teachers for language data. Teachers have for a long time recognized the benefits of working with real English in the classroom. This sampler provides up-to-date language data in the manageable form of concordances. These are one-line examples of a word in context, that have been taken from a vast collection of real English texts.

By studying the language in concordance form, learners at all levels can discover the central and typical patterns of English - what we actually say and write. In this way, they are able to recognize words which commonly go with a particular word. Providing learners with several examples of a word can also help them to learn the grammatical features of that word.

This collection provides learners with over 2000 real examples, all taken from the COBUILD Bank of English. The concordance lines have been chosen from a number of different sources, including newspapers, books, radio broadcast material, and both formal and informal spoken language.

The material complements the reference book Collins COBUILD English Guides: 5 Reporting. Although the concordance sampler can be used on its own, learners will gain additional benefit from referring to the Guide, which gives very detailed information about reporting what other people say in English.

All the material in this book is photocopiable within an institution. It is recommended that highlighter pens be made available, so that learners can analyse the concordances more easily.

The Concordance Pages

The main part of this book is the sets of concordances on pages 14-63. These start with concordances for the four most frequent reporting verbs: say, tell, ask and think. The rest of the concordances are arranged in alphabetical order of the keyword. Most of the keywords are reporting verbs (e.g. **explain**), but there are also a few reporting nouns (e.g. **advice**) and some which show particular patterns associated with reporting (e.g. **as**).

There is a complete list of the concordances on the Contents page. There is also information about each concordance on pages 10-13 in the Guide to the Concordance Pages. This information includes whether the lines have been left-sorted or right-sorted: that is, whether the lines are ordered alphabetically down the page according to the nearest word to the left or the right of the keyword. Many of the pages in this sampler have been right-sorted, in order to highlight the structures which often follow the keyword. Left-sorted pages illustrate the kinds of subjects which appear with certain reporting verbs. A few concordance pages contain unsorted lines, to allow learners more freedom in discovering patterns and collocations for themselves.

The Exercises

There are 5 worksheets, on pages 5-9, which offer different types of practice, including some helping the learners to get used to working with concordances in general. The worksheets can generally be used with any of the concordance pages and are suitable for learners of intermediate level and above.

The Guide to the Concordance Pages

The entries on pages 10-13 deal with each concordance page in turn. The information generally focuses on the different report structures shown. In some cases, there is also information about the different meanings or uses of the keyword. The line numbers of relevant examples are given for reference in each case. The concordance lines have been chosen to show the variety of ways in which the keyword is used, and also to give an idea of the relative frequency of the different ways. For example, in reporting, **order** is more frequently used with a noun group and a 'to'-infinitive clause following than with a 'that'-clause; and the concordance examples reflect this.

Exercises

1 Getting used to concordances - understanding the content

When you first look at concordances, it can be confusing because each line has a different example, often on a completely different subject - and many of the lines do not even show the whole sentence. Before you try to use these concordances to find out about report structures, you may find it useful to do a few exercises simply to help you get used to looking at concordances.

First, you need to get used to understanding or guessing what a line is about. You don't have to understand exactly what the topic is (sometimes it is impossible, anyway): you just need a rough idea. For example, where do you think the actions of the following sentences take place? How easy is it to guess? Underline the main words that help you to guess.

```
1    up a tiny vacant table at the open window of Pierre's cafe, ordered himself an ice-cream and Irish coffee, and sat back
2    n the earlier erroneous FBI reports. Although the judge had ordered all televisions removed from the jurors' motel room
3    he landlord had found out that she had deceived him and had ordered her to vacate her apartment. She had promised this
4    ational, an engine overheated. As a precaution, the captain ordered it shut down. None of the aircraft's passengers wer
5    r bodies to move their thin blood. As dawn broke the guards ordered everyone to their feet. Some didn't get to their fe
```

Look at any page of concordances. Note down briefly where the action takes place or what the situation is. Write the main words or clues which help you to guess.

LINE NUMBER	SITUATION	CLUES

© HarperCollins*Publishers* Ltd. 1995

2 Getting used to concordances - identifying the important parts of examples

When you are looking at concordances of report structures, you are often interested in what kind of structure the key word appears in. In many cases, it is fairly easy to see which parts of examples are useful for this purpose and which parts are probably less useful. The main part of the following concordance line for **claim** is underlined:

```
1    velling, some witnesses said later, at 60 miles an hour. He claimed he was driving at 50, in a 30 mph zone. He crossed o
```

The underlined sentence shows the report structure in full (a 'that'-clause). Underline the parts of the following concordance lines that make up the report structure. Note that you do not always need to underline a complete sentence.

```
2    imagined them formless and torpid. 'It would explode,' she claimed hopefully. 'Now you are imagining it on an electrica
3    ys that it is 14, and the other who swears blind that Denis claims it to be 20. I can see four possibilities: Denis is p
4    r example, a study of airline pilots found that the pilots claimed not to feel anxious or worried (indeed most said the
5    cause Pauling is a distinguished chemist, although he never claimed to be an expert on virus diseases such as colds, his
6    ing wealth. Many citizens grumble about this but few, Downs claims, would abolish bureaucracy if given the chance. ESCAL
```

Look at any concordance page for reporting verbs and identify the lines which show complete report structures. Write the structure below.

LINE NUMBER	REPORT STRUCTURE

3 Getting used to concordances - predicting missing parts of sentences

Sometimes, the report structure may be incomplete, especially at the end of the line; but you can often guess what the structure is, even though you may not be able to guess the actual words that are missing. The 'that'-clause (with a partial quote) following **claimed** can be identified in the following example, even though it is incomplete:

```
1    istro bar and saw herself as being on stage. Allen Ginsberg claimed Liverpool was 'the centre of consciousness of the h
```

You can also guess that probably not much is missing from the structure - we have the subject and verb (Liverpool was) and the main part of the complement (the centre of consciousness). The structure could be complete after the last phrase, which might be something like of the human race.

Underline the parts of the following examples which show the (incomplete) report structure and decide what structure is shown. Can you guess roughly how much is missing, and what the content of the missing part might be?

```
2    er than the average Leaker imagines. He can often be heard claiming that 'anyone could act in the movies' or that 'dipl
3    ntroversy to the boil in the early part of this century. He claimed that Mars was covered with a spider's web of fine li
4     or of increasing his inputs. Were he to decrease them, he claimed, he would have to lower his standard of living drast
5    er design; the result is Wren Gothic, and St. Mary has been claimed as the 'earliest true Gothic Revival church in Londo
6     questing, driven, thought-dominated man of the West, they claim. He is a total being, whose mere persistence in being
```

Look at the concordance page that you used for Exercise 2. How many lines start or finish with an incomplete structure? How many of these are part of the same report structure as the keyword? If they are part of the same structure, note down what kind of structure it is. Guess roughly how much is missing and what the content of the missing part might be.

LINE NUMBER	INCOMPLETE STRUCTURE	MISSING PART

4 Studying reporting structures

Often the important information about the structure follows the verb (e.g. the verb may be followed by a reported 'that'-clause), which is why the concordances are mostly right-sorted. However, in many cases, you need to look at what appears on both sides of the verb (e.g. a quote often comes before the reporting verb).

Look at the examples below:

	WORDS TO THE LEFT	VERB	WORDS TO THE RIGHT
1	they didn't want to	admit	that the prisoners existed
2	Teresa Stangl	admits	she was terribly angry
3	'I don't remember your name,' he	admitted	
4	'Can't say that I do,'	admitted	the Lieutenant
5	I thought about this, then	admitted:	'I don't know.'
6	She	admitted	meeting him on the day of the hare-hunt
7	Grandfather	admitted	taking it
8	he	admitted	to the crime
9	Meehan now	admitted	to being with another man
10	Penny Vincenzi	admits	relief

You can see from the above table that **admit** is used with 'that'-clauses (1, 2) and with quotes (3, 4, 5). It is also followed by -'ing' clauses (6, 7), by the preposition 'to' (8, 9) and by noun groups as objects (10). You can also see that it appears in different ways with quotes: it comes before or after the quote, and, if it comes after, the subject and verb are sometimes inverted ('admitted the Lieutenant'). Sometimes it is not easy to decide or describe what the structure is. Are the following concordance lines examples of one of the structures above, or are they completely different structures? How many kinds of report structures does **admit** appear in?

	WORDS TO THE LEFT	VERB	WORDS TO THE RIGHT
11	This programme will, Livingstone	admits,	double the rates
12	art galleries which Gertrude	admitted	she scarcely knew
13	seems much younger than he	admits	to.
14	[he] publicly	admitted	himself to be in the wrong

Look through the concordance page for **admit**, putting a letter (see Answers on page 64 which refer to 11-14 above) against each line to show which structure appears in that example. If any do not fit these groups, decide what the new structure is. If you cannot identify the structure, put 'x'. Check in the COBUILD Guide on Reporting or the COBUILD English Dictionary to see if all the structures you have identified are mentioned. Fortunately, not all reporting verbs are used in as many ways as **admit**; but you will quite often find that the concordance examples do not fit easily into the simple grammatical structures that most grammar books describe. Most of the pages of concordances are based on reporting verbs. Use any of these pages to look for the report structures in which these verbs are used.

You can use a similar table to the one for **admit** to help you identify the structures for other reporting verbs.

5 Looking at who says what

One aspect of report structures is that they may include or leave out information about who is speaking (or writing) to whom. For example, underline the speakers and/or hearers in the following concordance lines for **threaten**.

```
1   nstead, my mother protected me from the world and my father threatened me with it. My feeling of inadequacy increased s
2    and once to the military-registration office, where he was threatened with the loss of his pension if he did not curta
3   stion for a long time, and eventually he only agreed when I threatened to resign. Much as I liked and admired Frank, I
4    was. If there was going to be a power-cut tomorrow, as was threatened, then it would be sensible to get a camper's sto
```

From these examples, can you start to make rules about mentioning or leaving out the speaker and hearer with **threaten**? Look at the rest of the concordance page for **threaten** and see if the other lines support your rules.

Look at any other concordance page for reporting verbs and try to make the same kind of rules for that verb.

LINE NUMBER	SPEAKER	HEARER	STRUCTURE

Guide to the Concordance Pages

said RIGHT-SORTED
The most frequent reporting verb.
It is used in a number of different report structures, including:
    with a quote, eg 3, p14
    with a 'that'-clause, eg 28, p14
    in the middle of a reported main clause, eg 24, p14, or at the end of a reported main clause, eg 21, p14
    with a noun group as object, eg 1, p14
See also the concordance pages for **is** and **it**.
Say can be used with a non-human 'speaker' eg 19, p14.

say RIGHT-SORTED
The examples show **say** used in different phrases and fixed expressions, including:
    I dare **say**, eg 4
    say (for example), eg 5
    that is to **say**, eg 10
    all I can **say** is, eg 21
Most of these are used to introduce or comment on the speaker's own words.

told RIGHT-SORTED
Tell is used in a wide range of different report structures, including:
    with a 'that'-clause, eg 4, p17
    with a 'to'-infinitive clause, eg 12, p17
    followed by a prepositional phrase, eg 5, p17
    with a quote, eg 15, p17
    with a noun group as object, or as subject of a passive form, eg 1, p17
The hearer is mentioned in most cases when **tell** is used, though it may be the subject of a passive form, eg 6, p17.
In a few cases, the hearer is not mentioned, eg 35, p17.

tell RIGHT-SORTED
Two main meanings of **tell** are illustrated here:
    Say something to someone, eg 2
    Be able to know or judge the truth about events, eg 9
Many of the examples show **tell** being used in phrases and fixed expressions, including:
    I **tell** a lie, eg 1
    To **tell** you the truth, eg 35
    I'll **tell** you what, eg 37
Most of these involve the first meaning of **tell** given above, and they are used to introduce or comment on the speaker's own words.

asked RIGHT-SORTED
Ask is used to report especially questions and commands. It is used in many different report structures, including:
    with a quote, eg 3, p20
    with a 'wh-'clause, eg 13, p20
    with an 'if/whether'-clause, eg 14, p20
    with a 'to'-infinitive clause, eg 24, p20
    followed by a prepositional phrase, eg 2, p20
    with a noun group as object, eg 1, p20
In some cases, the hearer is mentioned, eg 4, p20, in other cases not, eg 38, p20.

ask, asking RIGHT-SORTED
Many of the examples show **ask** being used in phrases and fixed expressions, including:
    you may **ask,** eg 3
    if you **ask** me, eg 13
    Don't **ask** me, eg 15
    asking for trouble, eg 28
    I was only **asking,** eg 37
Most of these are used to introduce or comment on the speaker's own words.

thought RIGHT-SORTED
Think is used in two main ways:
    to report words passing through a person's mind, eg 16, p23
    to talk about someone's opinion, eg 6, p23
In some of the examples, it is not completely clear which of these two meanings is involved, eg 2, p23.
When **think** is used with quotes, eg 7, p23, or indirect quotes, eg 8, p23, only the first meaning is involved.
Think is also used with other structures, including:
    with a 'that'-clause, eg 6, p23
    followed by a prepositional phrase, eg 4, p23
    with a noun group as object followed by a complement, eg 20, p23.

think LEFT-SORTED
Many of the examples show **think** being used in phrases and fixed expressions, including:
    I **think,** eg 4
    I should **think,** eg 16
    Don't you **think,** eg 39
These are all connected with giving your opinion or checking about the hearer's opinion. When your opinion is negative, you can make **think** negative instead of the verb in the reported clause, eg 2.
In many cases, the clause with **think** can appear at the beginning of the sentence, eg 6; or in the middle, eg 13; or at the end, eg 7.

according to, allegedly, apparently, to quote, in the words of RIGHT-SORTED
These are all reporting adjuncts (see also **as**).
according to can be used with full quotes, eg 7; or partial quotes, eg 1; or with reports, eg 3.
in the words of and **to quote** are normally used with full quotes, eg 32; or partial quotes, eg 37.
apparently and **allegedly** are not normally used with quotes. They are used when you want to signal that you are saying what someone else has told you, but you don't say who that person is.
The adjuncts can all appear in different positions in the report structure, especially **apparently** and **allegedly.**

add, begin, continue, go on, interrupt, mention RIGHT-SORTED
These are all reporting verbs that show how the reported message fits in with the rest of the language event.
add is often used with quotes, eg 1; but it can be used with 'that'-clauses, eg 6
begin, **continue**, **go on** and **interrupt** are normally used (in reporting) with quotes, eg 10, 17, 24, 32
mention is often used with 'that'-clauses, eg 38; but it can be used in other structures as well, eg 35.

admit RIGHT-SORTED
A reporting verb (it has another main meaning: if you **admit** someone, you allow them to enter).
It is used in a number of different report structures, especially:
    with a 'that'-clause, eg 36
    with a quote, eg 8
    with an '-ing' clause, eg 18
    followed by a prepositional group with 'to', eg 39
    with a noun group as object, eg 22, or as subject of a passive form, eg 40
    followed by a noun group + 'to'-infinitive clause, eg 12.

advice, announcement, assurance, claim, comment, information RIGHT-SORTED
These are all reporting nouns.
All can be followed by a 'that'-clause, eg 2, 11, 17, 22, 34, 37
All can also be followed by a prepositional phrase, eg 9, 16, 21, 33
advice and **claim** can be followed by a 'to'-infinitive clause, eg 6, 25
They can sometimes be used with quotes, eg 31
See also **order.**

advise RIGHT-SORTED
This is a reporting verb, used in a number of different report structures, including:
   with a 'to'-infinitive clause (the hearer is always mentioned), eg 7
   with a quote, eg 16
   with a 'that'-clause, eg 38
   followed by a prepositional phrase, eg 4
   followed by a noun group as object, eg 1
   with an '-ing' clause, eg 10.

answer, reply RIGHT-SORTED
These are both reporting verbs which show that the speaker is responding to a previous question.
They can both be used in a number of different report structures, including:
   with a quote, eg 6, 27
   with a 'that'-clause, eg 18, 34
   followed by a prepositional phrase with 'with', eg 12, 39
   with no information about the message, eg 4, 29
In addition, **answer** can be used with a noun group as object, eg 2; and **reply** can be used with a prepositional group with 'to', eg 38.

apologize, nag, quarrel, scold, tell off RIGHT-SORTED
These are all reporting verbs which not only show the speaker's purpose, but also give an idea of what was said. **Apologize**, **scold** and **tell off** can all be followed by a prepositional phrase with 'for' giving more information about what was said, eg 2, 31, 36.

as RIGHT-SORTED
The concordance lines show **as** used with reporting verbs in reporting adjuncts (see also **according to**). The examples show many of the verbs which are most frequently used in these adjuncts.
The '**as**'-clause adjuncts come at the beginning of the sentence, eg 1; or in the middle, eg 3; or - more rarely - at the end, eg 30.
When you use an '**as**'-clause adjunct, it normally means that you accept that what the speaker said is true.

bark, cackle, growl, grunt, roar, snarl, snort, whine RIGHT-SORTED
All of these are reporting verbs which show how the speaker spoke. They are verbs which can also be used to describe the noises made by animals.
They are normally used with quotes.
With some of them, you can emphasize the violence of the way of speaking by mentioning the hearer in a prepositional phrase with 'at', eg 3, 7, 19.
With some, you can emphasize the loudness of the way of speaking by using a phrasal verb with 'out', eg 5, 10, 21.
See also **laugh**, **shout**.

be UNSORTED
This concordance page shows the reporting verbs which can be followed by a 'that'-clause with the verb in the base form (sometimes called the subjunctive). To show this more clearly, examples have been chosen where the verb in the reported clause is **be**.
Reporting nouns related to these reporting verbs can also be followed by the same kind of clause, eg 3.
These report structures are used when you are reporting orders, suggestions or requests.

believe RIGHT-SORTED
Believe is used in two main ways:
   to talk about someone's opinion, eg 3, 4
   to report what someone accepts as true, eg 1, 26
In some of the examples, it is not completely clear which of these two meanings is involved, eg 5.
It is usually the first meaning which is involved when the reported clause is a 'that'-clause, eg 8; or when the clause with **believe** comes in the middle of the reported clause, eg 15; or when the reported clause is a 'to'-infinitive clause, eg 32. In these cases, **believe** is very similar to think.
It is usually the second meaning which is involved when **believe** is followed by a noun group as object, eg 1; or by a prepositional phrase with 'in', eg 11.

claim RIGHT-SORTED
This is a reporting verb which shows that you do not necessarily accept that what the speaker said is true.
It is used in a number of different report structures, including:
   with a 'that'-clause, eg 27
   in the middle of a reported main clause, eg 1, or at the end of a reported main clause, eg 12
   with a 'to'-infinitive clause, eg 30
   with a quote, eg 16
   with a noun group as object, eg 3.

congratulate, bless, compliment, praise RIGHT-SORTED
These are all reporting verbs which not only show the speaker's purpose, but also give an idea of what was said. When you use these verbs, you mention the target (the person or thing spoken about); and the verbs show that something good was said about the target.
They can all be followed also by a prepositional phrase giving more information about what was said. The prepositions used include 'for', eg 2; 'on', eg 21; or 'upon', eg 5.
See also **criticize**.

criticize, abuse, blame, charge, condemn RIGHT-SORTED
These are all reporting verbs which not only show the speaker's purpose, but also give an idea of what was said. When you use these verbs, you mention the target (the person or thing spoken about); and the verbs show that something bad was said about the target.
They can all be followed also by a prepositional phrase giving more information about what was said. The prepositions used include especially 'for', eg 7; and 'as', eg 36.
With **blame** you can mention the cause of the bad event in a prepositional phrase with 'on', eg 23.
With **charge** you can mention the bad event in a prepositional phrase with 'with', eg 32.
See also **congratulate**.

demand RIGHT-SORTED
This is a reporting verb which can be used in a number of different report structures, including:
   with a quote, eg 1
   with a 'that'-clause where the verb in the reported clause is in the base form (the subjunctive - see also **be**), eg 26
   with a 'that'-clause where the verb in the reported clause has a modal (often 'should'), eg 24
   with a 'to'-infinitive clause, eg 31
   with a noun group as object, eg 2.

describe, call, define, refer RIGHT-SORTED
These are all reporting verbs which draw attention to the words that the speaker used to talk about something or someone. They are all often used with partial quotes, eg 1, 14, 26, 33.
With **describe**, **define** and **refer**, you use a prepositional phrase with 'as' to mention the words that the speaker used, whether or not these words are given in a partial quote, eg 3, 25, 35.
With **refer**, you always use a prepositional phrase with

'to' to mention the thing or person that the speaker talked about.
With **call**, you use a noun group as object to mention the thing or person that the speaker talked about and a noun group as complement to mention the words the speaker used, eg 15; you can also use an adjective as complement, eg 20.

emphasize RIGHT-SORTED
This is a reporting verb which is used in a number of different report structures, including:
   with a noun group as object, eg 1, or as subject of a passive form, eg 16
   with a 'that'-clause, eg 21
   in the middle of a reported main clause, eg 40
   with a 'wh'-clause reporting an exclamation, eg 13
   with a quote, eg 39 (this is not as common as the other report structures).

explain RIGHT-SORTED
This is a reporting verb which is used in a number of different report structures, including:
   with a quote, eg 6
   with a 'that'-clause, eg 9
   in the middle of a reported main clause, eg 4, or at the end of a reported main clause, eg 19
   followed by a prepositional phrase with 'about', eg 1
   with a noun group as object, eg 10
   with a 'wh'-clause summarising the message, eg 38.

give, deliver, issue, make, offer RIGHT-SORTED
These are all verbs which can be used with reporting nouns. The combination of verb plus reporting noun functions in a similar way to a reporting verb: eg the example in line 1 could be expressed as 'Dad finally warned them not to look').
The concordance lines show a number of the reporting nouns with which each verb frequently appears. Some combinations are fairly fixed phrases, eg 8; whereas in others the same reporting noun appears with different verbs, eg 7, 40.

go, have it, run LEFT-SORTED
These are reporting verbs which are used to report the words of non-human 'speakers'.
The concordance examples show the kinds of reporting situations in which you commonly use the verbs. For example,
   you can use **go** when you report what a story says, eg 11
   you can use **have it** when you report what a legend says, eg 22

you can use **run** when you report what a newspaper headline says, eg 30.

insist RIGHT-SORTED
This is a reporting verb which has two main meanings:
   say very strongly that something is true, eg 1
   say very strongly that something must be done, eg 9
It is used in a number of different report structures. In some of these structures, it may have either of the two meanings above:
   with a quote, eg 1
   with a 'that'-clause, eg 4
   in the middle of a reported main clause, eg 2; or at the end of a reported main clause, eg 36
In some structures, **insist** only has the second meaning above.
   with a 'that'-clause where the verb in the reported clause has a modal (often 'must' or 'should'), eg 14
   followed by a prepositional group with 'on', eg 15; or 'upon', eg 39

is, are, was, were, been RIGHT-SORTED
This concordance page gives examples of a special reporting structure in which the reporting verb appears inside the reported message. The reporting verb is in a passive form, and is followed by a 'to'-infinitive. This structure is a way of avoiding mentioning the speaker. The page shows many of the reporting verbs which commonly appear in this structure.
See also **it**.

it UNSORTED
This concordance page gives examples of another structure which can be used to avoid mentioning the speaker (see also **is**). The reporting verb is in a passive form with introductory **it** as the subject.
With most of the reporting verbs that can appear in this structure, the message is given in a 'that'-clause, eg 1. With a few of the reporting verbs, the message is given in a 'to'-infinitive clause, eg 7.

laugh, gasp, groan, moan, sigh, sob RIGHT-SORTED
All of these are reporting verbs which show how the speaker spoke. They refer to the speaker's general behaviour as they spoke, especially the other noises they made (for example **laughter**).
They are normally used with quotes, eg 1, although they are occasionally used with a 'that'-clause, eg 39.
See also **bark**, **shout**.

order RIGHT-SORTED
This is a reporting verb which is used in a number of different report structures, including:
   with a quote, eg 2
   with a noun group as object and a 'to'-infinitive clause, eg 9; the noun group can also appear as the subject of a passive form, eg 40
   with a 'that'-clause where the verb in the reported clause has a modal (often 'should' or 'must'), eg 26, or is in the base form (the subjunctive), eg 29
   with a noun group as object followed by a complement - the complement is often a past participle, eg 3, or a prepositional phrase or adverb of direction, eg 8
   with a noun group as object, eg 4

order, promise, proposal, request, suggestion RIGHT-SORTED
These are all reporting nouns.
They can all be followed by a 'to'-infinitive clause, eg 4, 9, 21, 29, 39.
They can also all be followed by a 'that'-clause, eg 1, 8, 17, 27, 34.
All except **promise** can be followed by a 'that'-clause where the verb in the reported clause is in the base form (the subjunctive), eg 3, 18, 25, 37.
promise and **suggestion** can be followed by a prepositional phrase with 'of', eg 10, 32.
proposal and **request** can be followed by a prepositional phrase with 'for', eg 16, 24.
See also **advice**.

persuade, convince, dissuade RIGHT-SORTED
These are reporting verbs which show the effect of what the speaker said on the hearer. The hearer is always mentioned, either as the object, or as the subject of a passive form.
When the effect on the hearer is to make him or her carry out an action, **persuade** and **convince** are normally followed by a 'to'-infinitive clause, eg 2, 22. In this case, **persuade** is more often used than **convince**.
When the effect is to change the hearer's opinion, **persuade** and **convince** are normally followed by a 'that'-clause, eg 5, 24. In this case, **persuade** often implies that the speaker had to try very hard to change the hearer's opinion, and perhaps did not succeed, whereas **convince** usually implies that the speaker was definitely successful.
When the effect is to change the hearer's opinion, both **persuade** and **convince** can also be followed by a prepositional phrase, eg 1, 21.

© HarperCollins*Publishers* Ltd. 1995

Dissuade is used with a prepositional phrase with 'from', eg 38.
The verbs can be used without giving information about the effect on the hearer, eg 16, 36.

point out RIGHT-SORTED
This is a reporting phrasal verb which shows that you accept that what the speaker said is true.
It is used in a number of different report structures, including:
    with a quote, eg 4
    with a 'that'-clause, eg 23
    in the middle of a reported main clause, eg 3; or at the end of a reported main clause, eg 34
    followed by a noun group as object, eg 1
point out is also often used in 'as'-clause adjuncts (see **as**).

promise RIGHT-SORTED
This is a reporting verb which is used in a number of different report structures, including:
    with a quote, eg 15
    with a 'to'-infinitive clause, eg 40
    with a 'that'-clause, eg 31
    with a noun group as object, eg 1
In all these structures, the hearer may be mentioned, eg 10; or not, eg 1.

prove, demonstrate, show LEFT-SORTED
These are reporting verbs which show the result of what the speaker said. The results are not actions or opinions (see **persuade**), but facts.
The 'speaker' may be a person, eg 8, 17, 30; but in many cases the 'speaker' is a text, eg 20; or, most frequently, something abstract such as research or evidence, eg 1, 19, 29.

put it RIGHT-SORTED
This is a reporting verb phrase which is used to draw attention to the way the speaker expressed his or her ideas.
It is often used with an adverb or prepositional phrase referring to manner, eg 8, 12; or with a noun group with the word 'way', eg 1, 5.
It is also often used in an 'as'-clause adjunct (see **as**).
The clause with **put it** is used to introduce a quote, eg 7; or a reported main clause, eg 5.
The clause with **put it** may come before the message, eg 6; or in the middle, eg 10; or at the end, eg 25.

remind RIGHT-SORTED
This is a reporting verb which is used in a number of different report structures, including:
    with a 'that'-clause, eg 4 (in this case, the speaker is making the hearer remember a fact)
    with a 'to'-infinitive clause, eg 7 (in this case, the speaker is making the hearer remember to do something)
    with a quote, eg 3
    followed by a prepositional phrase with 'of', eg 13; or 'about', eg 2
The hearer is always mentioned, even if there is no information about the message, eg 16.

shout, cry, mutter, exclaim, scream, whisper, yell RIGHT-SORTED
These are all reporting verbs which show how loudly or quietly the speaker spoke.
They are all used with quotes, eg 2, 9, 15, 21, 25, 30, 35.
They are also sometimes used with 'that'-clauses, eg 22, 27, 31.
When the message is an order, **shout** and **yell** are used with 'to'-infinitive clauses, eg 7, 36.
If you want to emphasize the violence of the speaker's way of speaking, you can mention the hearer in a prepositional phrase with 'at', eg 1, 35.

so, not LEFT-SORTED
This concordance page shows how you can use **so** and **not** following a reporting verb to avoid repeating a message that you have already reported.
The examples show many of the reporting verbs which are frequently used with **so** and **not** in this way. Only two of the verbs are genuine reporting verbs which refer to what someone said - '**say**' and '**tell**'. The other verbs report people's opinions. '**Say**' and '**tell**' are not used in this way with **not**.

suggest RIGHT-SORTED
This is a reporting verb which is used in a number of different report structures, including:
    with a quote, eg 2
    with a 'that'-clause, eg 20
    with a 'that'-clause where the verb in the reported clause has a modal (often 'should'), eg 21; or is the base form (or subjunctive), eg 24
    in the middle of a reported main clause, eg 3
    followed by an '-ing' clause, eg 9
    with a noun group as object, eg 1; or as subject of a passive form, eg 36
In most cases, the hearer is not mentioned; but if he or she is mentioned you use a prepositional phrase with 'to', eg 38.

threaten RIGHT-SORTED
This is a reporting verb which is used in a number of different report structures, including:
    with a 'to'-infinitive clause, eg 20 (in this case, the hearer is not mentioned)
    with a prepositional phrase with 'with', eg 4 (in this case the hearer is mentioned)
    with a 'that'-clause, eg 2, 16 (in this case the hearer may or may not be mentioned)
    with a noun group as object, eg 12
    with no information about the message, eg 6, 7

warn RIGHT-SORTED
This is a reporting verb which is used in a number of different report structures, including:
    with a quote, eg 5
    with a 'that'-clause, eg 8
    with a 'to'-infinitive clause, eg 4
    with a prepositional phrase with 'about', eg 6; or 'against', eg 2
    with no information about the message, eg 38
In most of these structures, the hearer is usually mentioned (with a 'to'-infinitive clause the hearer is always mentioned). Sometimes, however, the hearer is not mentioned, especially with quotes, eg 17.

wish RIGHT-SORTED
This reporting verb is used in two main ways:
    to report what someone hopes, eg 1
    to report what someone says, eg 3
In the second use, **wish** is followed by a noun group reporting the message, and the hearer is mentioned.
In the first use, **wish** appears in a number of different report structures, including:
    with a 'that'-clause, eg 2
    with a 'to'-infinitive clause, eg 37
    followed by a noun group as object and a 'to'-infinitive clause, eg 15
    followed by a prepositional phrase with 'for', eg 7
    followed by a noun group as object, and a complement, eg 31
The verb forms in the reported clause following wish are very varied, depending on whether the **wish** refers to something that has already happened, eg 5; or to something in the present, eg 1; or to something in the future, eg 40.

said

1. that I could rely on the Englishness of the English. No one said a word. This was probably not from lack of curiosity.
2. id. 'How old do you think he is?' 'What he looks like,' Ned said. 'About fifteen, ain't he? Gone to Arkansaw? Then some
3. een said. 'You all ready?' he asked. 'Bags all packed,' she said. 'All I have to do is lock them.' Billy had an almost
4. of plant bargaining agreements. Mr Shanks' final paragraph said: 'All of this seems to me of great potential importanc
5. ng with the boy. 'It's on the third floor,' Mrs Fairweather said. 'All the way down the corridor, the last door to the
6. someone in my life who can drive a car.' 'I've forgotten,' said Anne. 'You were a demon driver once.' Anne had indeed
7. d. He didn't want to have to talk to his sister. She hadn't said anything that he wanted to hear since he was eight yea
8. hink so.' We sat in silence for a minute or two and then he said: 'Are you happy coming here?' 'Oh, yes ... Yes, quite.
9. I thought you'd never ask,' she said, as they went off. Dan said: 'Aren't you going to eat anything?' 'I seem to have b
10. ehind and work without covering any line of fire.' To me he said : ' Be careful not to move your hands or feet by the s
11. this was pretentious and academic in the wrong way. 'Well,' said Bill, 'you'd better let me read this work. Is there a
12. w eyes overlooked its back. 'How the hell did that happen?' said Brody. 'A car?' 'No, a man.' Ellen's breath came in so
13. e glasses. 'Five minutes ago. He just died.' 'I'm sorry,' I said. 'But no tears for Lonnie. His words, not mine. 'He ha
14. ow telegram envelope that was unopened; inside the telegram said `Confirming Monday. Have enough money with you. John.'
15. even-year-old daughter, Heidi, who one morning at breakfast said, 'Daddy, when I have an OK Daddy and an OK Mama, how c
16. was on beige, deckle-edged stationery. 'Dear Mr Morris,' it said, 'Donald will not be coming back to Cambridge this ter
17. stood up, the father made his usual joke. 'Be careful,' he said. 'Don't let those soldiers grab you. We don't have eno
18. d been responsible for her sister's death.' 'Good heavens!' said Dr Willoughby - 'surely you are not suggesting - ' 'Th
19. the lift, in silence. A roughly painted notice on the wall said, 'ENGLISH FACULTY VIGIL, DEALER STEPS 11 A.M.' As the
20. ts)) WASHINGTON - Secretary of State Alexander M. Haig Jr. said Friday that the United States is not ready to let Is
21. eceipts.' Liddy was among those who received the money, she said. 'Gordon's a case of loyalty to the President. He'll n
22. e to glimpse a porter grinning at his mate with a look that said 'Got it bad, ain't he?' Yet - or so it seemed to me -
23. er to regulate prices and production. The Conservatives, he said, had admitted as much in calling for high production t
24. t to mention anything which might upset me again. Tony, she said, had gone back to Newbury that afternoon. Gerald Kings
25. no feelings required but gratitude and joy. His class, Bill said, had tried to tell him that the statue represented a r
26. nexpected, was Haig, who called to leave a book in which he said he had written something. It was a volume of Haig's de
27. most instantly, it seemed, she was awakened by a voice that said, 'Hey there, are you okay?' She opened her eyes and sa
28. ther and dad told him not to believe all that stuff. But he said his grandmother whispered it was true anyway, so he be
29. st've known.' 'One can't do things like that.' 'Look,' Alan said, 'I don't mind for myself, all I have to do is shell o
30. dancing in the centres of them. 'Quite a long time ago,' he said, 'I saw a short medical film that had been brought ove
31. zled silence on the other end of the line. 'Well, now,' Dad said, 'I see you finally got smart.' I rented a car and dro
32. e in and said that as John was going I should also leave. I said I would prefer to stay for a few more months, and was
33. now,' I said. He handed it to me and I pointed it at him. I said, 'I'll certainly use this on you if you try any such t
34. 's important. It's a sport, not a study'. 'In that case', I said, 'I'm afraid I'm no sportsman'. 'No ? Then why have yo
35. efused to tell him what the trouble was. It could wait, she said. If it could wait, he thought, it couldn't be so bad.
36. e moved. His subchiefs and his sons objected, however. They said if the agency was moved, they would not go. Not even t
37. even for teenagers. Wow, I said. Can you imagine, my friend said, if they started handing out sentences like that over
38. baby we have. Will you take it as a standing invitation?' I said indeed I would, and that I looked forward to many happ
39. d fitted so snugly into the bottom. 'You're going out.' She said it mechanically, like one who is beyond surprise. 'Whe
40. her a part in The Lady's Not for Burning. He had hoped, he said, it might prove therapeutic for post-natal depression.

said

1. us statements. Magruder called about half an hour later and said it was 'absolutely untrue' that he received any money
2. left wrist to see what time the luminous hands of my watch said it was. They said it was 4.15. It says much for my men
3. you're giving yourself a title you haven't earned,' Rudolph said. 'Joke,' Gretchen said. 'Do you want a list? Beginning
4. ristmas and seemed to be hanging on all winter. 'Julie,' he said, 'let's go home.' She sat up straight on his lap, surp
5. ment of men. All principles, all truths, are relative, they said. 'Man is the measure of all things.' These were the fa
6. n rather to the scandal of doctrinal bickering, which, they said, many in the Church had been deploring for a long time
7. eer in which I have flourished.' 'I don't believe it, sir,' said Mr Bingham furiously. 'Don't believe what, sir?' 'That
8. my reward. 'You don't get rewarded for doing kind things,' said my sister. 'Everyone knows that. But I'd help you to l
9. reconsidered and nodded, and finally decided against it and said no. Though she had been three times married, Miss Harr
10. , asked whether he had been afraid of losing the battle, he said: 'Not of losing. But I was scared of what would happen
11. lcome her. 'We're glad to see you.' The woman, Mrs Hindley, said nothing, 'Do you recognise me? I live in your road,' L
12. Winifred averted her eyes from the figure in the bed. Bill said, 'Now, it's all right, now you can come home, and all
13. creeping in. In one of his earthy homilies, Khrushchev once said of specialists from the agricultural institutes, 'They
14. r lips. 'Almost always everything went like clockwork,' she said. 'One time the couple didn't show up. I called and the
15. lay ... No, I'm afraid I haven't, professor.' 'Oh dear,' he said pleasantly. 'Well, we shall just have to wait, then.'
16. re-enter the small world she had made for them. She had (he said) poisoned their minds against him. And it was true. Sh
17. what happened. I was glad. You believe me, Johnny? ' Johnny said reassuringly, 'Sure, Nino, I believe you.' Lucy and Ju
18. the remand system. It seems to me that quite a lot has been said recently about the state of our prisons, but that the
19. righton. Everybody said it was going to be a boy. Everybody said stop smoking, stop drinking, do this, do that. People
20. his wallet and put down five ten dollar bills. 'Enough?' he said. 'Thanks.' Rudolph put the bills carelessly in his poc
21. shorter than me and twice the weight. So I thanked him and said that I had decided to wear my Good Suit after all. I w
22. to our strictly illegal communication. On this day, Melanie said that she had a postcard from Sheila, and did I want to
23. ' The following afternoon the boy's mother called me up and said that she had received a phone call from Uncle Dick. So
24. t life and education is a part of that process. It is often said that we are only young once and this, of course is tru
25. e graph-lined page were fat letters in pencil. 'Dear Girl,' said the letters, 'I love you.' I read the message and star
26. witnesses—and even ordered that some evidence be shredded. Said the report: 'The direction on the part of the chief wa
27. to be gracious and charming. 'One more thing, Mr Kleiber,' said the voice at the other end. 'I am responsible for Mr K
28. e took out a gun and gave it to Lampone. 'Use this one,' he said. 'They can never trace it. Leave it in the car with Pa
29. nt room to my mum. Then she came running to the kitchen and said, 'They're here.' I said, 'Who's here,' and she said, '
30. pologise to him, I suppose.' 'It might be a good idea.' She said this in a tone that made him turn his back for a momen
31. lived and visited her. It's quite simple.' 'But Gertrude,' said Tim, 'have you known about this for a long time - ?' '
32. to supper one night after the play by himself. Lady Tree is said to have looked in at the door and said: 'The port's on
33. At the end of the Ballet, I found other seats. My companion said to me, 'What would you do if one of your kids from Sum
34. chols said. One more sweep of the beam. 'Miss Saunders,' he said to the secretary, 'can you come inside for a moment, p
35. ls, tried to make him drink, sat over him. The psychiatrist said to Winifred that the root cause of Marcus's troubles a
36. ' ' Shall I stop?' I volunteered. At the same time, a voice said: 'What about little Peggy here? Had she better come wi
37. or I did, or my sister did, and everyone was very happy and said what we had each been doing during the day. The room w
38. n't take them back to the shop. I phoned Johnson's and they said, yes, you had ordered them. Philip, is anything the ma
39. es ago?' 'What you wanted,' Dan said. 'Weren't we?' Barbara said: 'You have been thinking, haven't you?' 'That's right,
40. my sent me the articles, together with a letter in which he said: 'You see, it is useless for me to try to compromise w

say

1. res from generation to generation. Ours was a - how shall I say? - a kind of mound of translucent stone, perhaps quartz
2. t by now we tend to shrug and say: Well, you know what they say about setting a thief to catch a thief. The Senate co
3. think I fight for your benefit, Father?' 'Well, I wouldn't say 'benefit.'' But of course, who could tell what he was t
4. unt them. It's a bad habit, is counting them.' 'Yes, I dare say, but how many do you think it was? Roughly.' 'Ooh ... s
5. ay in which actors perform their duties. Given the role of, say, Claudius in Hamlet, they tacitly judge the character a
6. al arguments raged, it turned into a fairly serious, not to say dangerous affair. He's matured as a player, particularl
7. water onto the dry flowers. 'Am I? Yes, I suppose I am.' 'I say!' Donald said, 'I'd rather like to wait and see how lon
8. entioned at the trial. 'As to Mr Hearst,' he wrote, 'I dare say he first saw the lines when all this hullabaloo directe
9. that made him pause were ones of how and when. No one could say he was not practical, for he gave continual thought to
10. ny approach. The addict's reaction to his habit, that is to say his or her alleged reaction, varies according to sophis
11. . That, certainly, and their uncomfortable attitude, not to say his silliness as he laid her head against his, must ens
12. into the side of the hole. Much quicker that way.' 'I must say I can't see the need for haste,' said Dr Board' 'I shou
13. a Dr Anita Johnson - who was soon flown back, I am glad to say. I had little notion of what object the expedition was
14. me at all on what led to it or what led up to it, shall we say. I have no actual friends who were friends in common wi
15. the deacon, 'you'll get those who can't stop, as you might say. I remember a man who went on for over an hour and so s
16. 'Well?' he asked. Mr Roberts shifted his long legs. 'Can't say I took it all in,' he confessed. 'Nor me,' admitted Mr
17. le every morning ran out of coffee.' 'Is that true?' 'Sure. Say, I want to thank you for sending your drummer in.' 'It
18. while. A touch of his old good humor returned: 'Let's just say I'll be willing to put the blossoming situation in peri
19. ' he said. 'How far you've failed, of course, is for you to say. I've never met a parent with the face to claim he'd ac
20. s fine if it's carried out in the right spirit - that is to say, if the parent is really trying not to fuss or worry ab
21. his chair as if tired, he closed his eyes. 'Then all I can say is that I don't understand you,' he said heavily. My ne
22. you're about it, get the downstairs loo working. All I can say is things had better improve because I don't think I ca
23. ed to go back to that place?' 'Oh, well, you know what they say: lightning never strikes twice in the same place.' 'I w
24. Jefferson had used the same argument with him. Needless to say, Madison was as appalled as I and dissuaded Jefferson f
25. terms,' adds Howard, 'we've redefined it internally.' 'I'll say,' says Barbara. When the new academic year came around
26. to see you don't give her any more of it, that's all I can say.' She went out, and Albert watched her through the open
27. their rockers,' shouted Mr Morris. 'Merely, well, shall we say, slightly unbalanced.' 'That's not what the police say
28. s what they do.' 'You don't like the Cav much?' 'I wouldn't say that.' Far up the strip, 400 metres away, there was a m
29. 've always fought against this and I always will but I must say that it's getting better, things are improving. On the
30. , that is. Well, by way of thoughtful reacting, I can only say that things are bad and they'll probably get worse. The
31. ly want to know. How can a man who wrote a book like, let's say, The Fenlanders, or built a building like the Roper Hou
32. rent matter. I do not like to see a book with the title of, say, The History of Progressive Schools when such a book ig
33. 'Dakotans failed totally to get themselves together. Sad to say, the only North Dakotans left are three maiden ladies i
34. 'Watch out. I ain't near done talking yet—if I'm a mind.' 'Say the word,' Butch said. 'I'll beat the hell out of him j
35. very few of them really know their business. That is not to say they won't make money for their angels on odd occasions
36. cstasy (although, having been to the clouds, I can honestly say they're a nice place to visit but I wouldn't want to li
37. At the table, I mean.' 'I'm not married.' 'Go on! You don't say! There's time, though.' The grocer glanced towards the
38. e has already realized, can end only so. The Sister, I dare say, was surprised, having naturally assumed that I would n
39. ack.' 'From the top of your profession?' 'Big deal. As they say.' We began to run. 'Actually I've been here about a TV
40. be, that stuff looks like sunshine out there. What did you say your name was?' 'Anne Cavidge.' 'Never heard of you. Do

told

1. tch for twenty-seven years, and many colourful stories were told about him. Born in Yorkshire, he had come to South Afr
2. way or the other. In defiance of everything that I had been told about not camping next to streams - because of the dan
3. saved ...? She wanted desperately to finish the novel, she told Alexis. Yet she couldn't write. It was easier to plan
4. t come back to the flat, though they met there and Gertrude told Anne that Tim had gone and it was over. They did not d
5. m his night reading. 'A drowning,' he said, embarrassed. He told Brody about the phone call from Foote. 'I didn't know
6. find a woman who doesn't know how to care for a car,' I was told by the Automobile Association, 'but for every woman yo
7. nearly fast enough. Mel wanted his children to grow up (he told Cindy) with the knowledge that they were equal to othe
8. n't let up on her listening smile, but at the same time she told Clarissa, 'The curtain's not drawn properly.' Through
9. days,' she said helplessly. Marsha kept on crying. Lynn had told Derek she wouldn't be long, but she leaned against the
10. ations.' ' Well, actually, that was already done. You see I told Father that I was sure that you would come because, af
11. s, talked a great deal about himself and his own people. He told Francois how his father had died some thirty-five days
12. rive the gang to erect their barricades in Thames Street. I told Fred to divide his gang into two halves, and to send o
13. rday too Irene Cameron went round to Holyrood Crescent. She told Griffiths she wanted to go out and buy some clothes, a
14. they began to plot their elopement, this time for good. She told Harold of their intention as soon as he arrived. Her d
15. ency.' 'Well, Henry is always tired when he gets home,' Eva told her. 'And I go out a lot.' 'I'm not surprised,' said S
16. en table, frowning. His wife asked, 'Sonny, what is it?' He told her calmly, 'They shot the old man.' When he saw the s
17. t the same as the day she died. This made him impatient. He told her, 'Get along now, my girl. You can't stay here fore
18. ell on the floor with a thud. She sat up. 'Who is dead?' He told her. He described it. 'Where is the letter?' she deman
19. d have killed her if I had stayed an instant longer. I have told her I cannot even see her for two months. She calls it
20. es you know are often the worst. That's all very well, Evie told her mother, it's not so easily arranged. And since it
21. touched your food. I'd better pack you some sandwiches'. I told her not to bother - that I could buy buns or sandwiche
22. a fish-bone had got in her throat. He gave her a crust and told her to chew it hard. 'Chew it,' he said, very loud. He
23. Judy. Still, I'd like you to know where to find me.' And he told her where he was staying. 'It's very Catholic and Iris
24. d long governed her housekeeping procedures. Her mother had told her, 'You never put a hat on a table or a coat on a be
25. detected a flicker of irony in Hooper's voice, but then she told herself, Don't be stupid - you're making things up. 'H
26. y, stopping often to look into shop windows. Of course, she told herself, she was not going to take the bus. It was day
27. ackie and Bell, Meehan asked Irene where she came from. She told him. Having a teenage daughter of his own, he suggeste
28. g of the machinations of selection procedure. Frank Worrell told him how lucky he had been to miss England: a Test defe
29. her so alone. 'Oh he's around somewhere,' Etta said. 'I've told him not to come in here - I can't stand him around, I
30. en you took over, came to power, ran the country.' 'Yes,' I told him, 'that would be quite nice.' 'It would mean a lot
31. - ask anybody - but I'm not exactly a mug. I called him in, told him to clear off and think himself lucky he wasn't in
32. yer, while Mr Bhoolabhoy waited outside. All the lawyer had told him was that Mr Pandey would be coming up on the after
33. all trouble less. I've been talking to the Superintendent - told him who you are and so on. He wouldn't commit himself,
34. white without turning silver. 'At the end of this year,' he told himself, 'I really am going to get out of this racket.
35. nglishman?' 'Yes.' Mrs Murray was followed by Mrs Boyle who told how Meehan had given assistance at the time of the Sco
36. entice. Who, pray, was Ginny today? Ginny was waiting to be told how nice it was of her to come all the way from Vermon
37. 'Outside?' 'Don't argue with me, George. Just do as you're told.' I am so sleepy I can hardly see to walk, but my moth
38. n and tap the corners gently,' he ordered. I did what I was told. I very nearly always found myself doing what he told
39. as proud to manage. 'I shall be off in a few minutes,' Lucy told Ibrahim. 'I've made another little list, because while
40. ough our letter-boxes as official letters and forms. We are told in different ways what to do, what to buy and how to t

told

1 ng. Don't bother to call on me or ring me or anything,' she told Judy. 'I mean it. I've given you up.' She rose from he
2 bout his answer. The next morning he arrived in the lab and told Max and John about his success. A few minutes later, B
3 ut whom the authorities were not sure. Before she left, she told me a bit about herself. She was in her late twenties,
4   point in arguing with him. I sat down and let him talk. He told me about his army experiences, and said that he was so
5   to give him a hint at least. He was here to do me good, he told me. He was eager to help me. 'I can put you into a goo
6 s trying to hide. When Josef was living in my apartment, he told me how they had kept him in solitary confinement durin
7   be done,' Eddie said. 'Why did it? You could have at least told me.' 'If I'd told you, it wouldn't have worked, would
8 ications to look for, I asked him what it was all about. He told me not to ask questions, just to do what I was told. F
9 eck it with you? You're in the bank almost every day, Erich told me so.' 'They check everything with me,' said Pitman.
10 dresses, were canned goods, eggs and cooking oil. My friend told me that she was a very fine cook. That she could reall
11 dering about in those hiils and that we should go north. He told me to give you the following instructions : 'You are a
12 asty turn. Did you put her there?' 'Sure. Sorry, boy. Mr S. told me to. Made an excuse to spike the bridge this morning
13 nerve on Christmas Day, 1968. He had been tempted, he later told me, to radio back from Apollo 8 that the crew had spot
14 geographers believed it'. I was astounded. Miss Bloomfield told me to wait for her and went out; a few minutes later s
15 I said I would, and he phoned Faubus's secretary, who, he told me, was a personal friend. He spoke at length into the
16 r? I wanted to go there on this trip. 'No, Professor,' they told me. 'We're very sorry, but there's a strict quarantine
17 he refused to begin until two men (his 'keepers', my father told me) were brought on to the platform to readjust his pi
18 ack to Switzerland. He told me what I had to do and then he told me what he was going to do. 'He said: 'There is only o
19 d, too!' 'Well, not a very big one, I'm afraid.' 'You never told me!' 'You don't mean to say you play the piano as well
20 r. I listened to her voice, watched the way she smiled, and told myself that these were the things that made her unique
21 spies? ' ' No, no, not spies. The boy in the story has been told not to go out of the garden, and ...' 'Who told him?'
22 carefully. 'You must never speak aloud in theatres,' I was told, 'otherwise somebody will overhear what you say and ma
23 ts are in this big house on the lake front.' He had already told Parker his important news but he wanted to enjoy it ag
24 he lake at the doorstep was deep. Reich and his wife simply told Peter that he should not go near the water. Having had
25 des. By the time they are four, children really enjoy being told stories. Television and radio proprammes enhance this;
26 ice. Here we received the housemistress's pep talk. We were told that if we made trouble we would get trouble, that if
27 vely house. Of course a wife can sometimes be a trial. I am told that Mrs. Monroe was so stuck-up that she had a platfo
28 to appeal and why. Send the letter within 28 days of being told the decision on your claim. You can ask the Citizens A
29 - to coop ourselves up any longer. 'Put your books away,' I told the delighted class, 'and we'll go out for a nature wa
30 the evidence of our efforts in glorious technicolor. I had told the hotel where I could be contacted and a phone call
31 ueen to allow her subjects to dress informally for Ascot. I told them how unattractive I thought my countrymen looked i
32 ng a very large idea. People asked if I could live there. I told them no, I couldn't live in China; it was not my count
33 is jacket. 'A hundred dollar bill saved my life once,' Reed told Thomas. He had been caught in a dreadful fire one nigh
34 ery rhyme went through my mind. I was shown into a room and told to wait there 'while I tell the mistress you're here'.
35 us if we wanted coffee. Vane said no, apologized, and then told us he had to leave for another meeting. 'I always have
36 Alec carrying helmets and boots. We didn't say a word. Matt told us later how they'd spent the whole day clinging to th
37 ctly what to wear, and having my meals set before me, being told when to get up and how to spend my entire day, my ever
38 the case. He knows he is adopted ... but he never has been told who his real mother was ... yes. Yes, I see ... Very w
39 a long trip but, so he claimed under drugs, he had not been told why. However, Kontarsky was in no mood to believe that
40 ell, what shall we do?' 'You could try Ebury Street.' 'I've told you, there isn't any Ebury Street any more. They've dr

tell

1 ast twenty years to fill Dame Edna Everage's whole house. I tell a lie. I wrote my first weekly letter in 1954 when I l
2 rtain cord. 'They swore me to silence. I promised I'd never tell a living soul.' He looked at Stein. 'Petrucci,' he sai
3 bothered me for years. Only you must promise you will never tell a soul what I am about to ask. I have two names. They
4 pounds. Though she tried to appear in high spirits, I could tell from the deep furrows in her forehead that she was dee
5 ted Tom. 'Well, the next time she mentions it, I wish you'd tell her from me to mind her own dam' business,' he cried a
6 s?' 'Certainly not, Mr Desland! Of course I wasn't going to tell him where you were. Actually I'm not at all sure where
7 nds which had been browned by the sun. 'There's not much to tell. I found Tim at his studio. Just him - there - he sai
8 s: if they do not say what they are trying to do nobody can tell if they fail. A good example of this was the British G
9 t, you know, for all that, it might not work. You can never tell in advance. They say only about thirty per cent make i
10 e,' Landy said. 'Can you see it?' ' Yes.' 'So far as we can tell, it is still in perfect condition. It's his right eye,
11 'There you are, you see.' 'Let's leave that,' Dixon said. 'Tell me: how long are you staying here this time?' 'For a f
12 ek. 'Well, really, and how long has it been going on? Don't tell me. I really believe it was love at first sight, wasn'
13 a bottle of scotch. He looked at me, pondering, then said: 'Tell me, my boy, do you think they have bars in heaven?' 'I
14 d the voice in his earphones. 'No. That's very interesting. Tell me, Professor Swallow, has anything like this ever hap
15 and optimism to persist, even when old friends said, 'Don't tell me you're still working on that?' How did she explain
16 ed. 'Only good can come. For everyone!' 'There's nothing to tell,' Mori insisted, and Yoshiko, looking at the bent-open
17 smile upon the vicar, that he felt quite young again, 'I'll tell Mr Temple that you're here.' The room was oppressively
18 tau? Frau Schreiber.' 'My God! I don't know, it was hard to tell; she had a lot of make-up on. Much younger than he was
19 ff your instruments, or unless you would like to be able to tell the time at night without switching on the bedside lam
20 p into the branches overhead. It's not very comfortable, to tell the truth. A twig is sticking him in the back. There i
21 tially. ` ... every time we did it, I made less mistakes. I tell you, a couple more visits from those Historical Depart
22 aid, 'that I cannot bear to lie in my bed without her. I'll tell you a secret, Rudolph. I wasn't at Jack and Jill's tha
23 .' 'I'll do it.' 'You've got to go to work.' 'I'll do it, I tell you.' After a moment she said, 'Ethan, I don't think I
24 'The doctors have been marvellous,' said Charlie. 'I can't tell you how marvellous. The personal attention. Where else
25 she seemed to have had Raymond in common. I said, 'I can't tell you how much I liked being in your house that evening.
26 f his hands. The sound it made was hard and brisk. 'I can't tell you how much it's done for me—our talk. I didn't expec
27 s the novel?' 'Stuck. Writing's harder than painting, I can tell you.' 'I expect it is.' 'Painters can just look at a
28 r there so bad is to save your necks from the Arabs. Let me tell you—I'm getting to Palestine all right and when I do I
29 st you. You might break the rules. You might turn honest. I tell you I'm scared.' I stood up and found my legs were hea
30 ving the old Spanish Conspiracy. And I've succeeded, let me tell you.' Indeed he had! To the end Don Carlos believed th
31 e it was asking for help and there were these fingers ... I tell you it was horrible. It didn't look natural.' 'No, wel
32 probably singing the same tune in my head. I don't have to tell you she was right. Allow me to mention, however, that
33 drink? You haven't any occupation except the bottle. Let me tell you something. I didn't miss you when you were away. I
34 r law and order exercises. Anyway, it woke Donald up, I can tell you. Talk about levitation!' 'You should have gone to
35 consulting me, 'It's fun for them to grow up together. 'To tell you the truth, Mother, the thought of a second child h
36 Mary. Suppose he's wrong. You'd be without protection.' 'I tell you this, Ethan, if you don't do it, I'll take the mon
37 'I can see that this is getting us nowhere,' I said. 'I'll tell you what, Clay. You calm down your friends for a few d
38 I said. Shapiro mused, the Stock fragrant on his breath. 'I tell you what,' he said. 'I'll go for a shooftie and sort h
39 ll me . . .' 'Yes, I do.' The hell with the business. 'I'll tell you what I'll do. I'll sit right here with you and wai
40 came from a spring and it was a treat after the pond, I can tell you! Worth going after. The dust from the roads in the

asked

1 soning. She looked thoughtful for the rest of our visit and asked a lot of questions about gardening and animal care an
2 the time remembering . . . He only came really alive when I asked about their kids. They got these two little girls - i
3 ter and thrust it into an envelope. 'And at what point,' he asked, 'are you going to spring the news on him and gather
4 their lunches cost more than 16 pounds a head. Marplan also asked businessmen how many hours they worked in an average
5 der why I carry on at all'. Since I was feeling friendly, I asked: 'But why do you get mixed up in all this semi-crooke
6 ingsley interrupted: 'We refuse to answer that.' 'But why?' asked Captain Burke. 'Everyone knows that's his full name.'
7 not the past.' ' 'Did he tell you he was an adopted child?' asked Celia. 'Yes, he did.' 'You see, what business is it r
8 ieve you were listening. What were you thinking about?' she asked. 'Cold sausage!' he remembered in triumph. Olivia als
9   help to housing and health insurance. In 1974 a BIM survey asked companies their reasons for providing cars. The resul
10 p to go to the kitchen. 'Well, what have you been up to?' I asked Dad. 'Jury duty,' he said. 'My first time. Have you e
11 'Not really. No.' 'Then how did you ...' 'A few weeks ago I asked Dawn Witherbie how her mother was and she told me she
12 ed a case he'd been reading about in The News of the World, asked Dixon's opinion on a clue in its prize crossword, and
13 nce, the others were inclined to think it a good plan. They asked each other why you shouldn't eat with a knife. The re
14 excited. The police drove up and down the streets and they asked everybody if they had seen the monster. The monster w
15 and sighed wonderingly. 'Who was he afraid of?' Liebermann asked. 'Everyone. People at the office, people who simply l
16 ere customers. Now they were all alert and jumping about. I asked for a cup of coffee, and no cup of coffee ever came t
17 ry to restore their self-possession. Mrs Davenport rang and asked for Emily to be sent. While less noticeable on state
18 in a 'recession' and questioned the original diagnosis; he asked for further tests to be taken in three months time. O
19 Goldsmith!). I knocked on the door of the nearest cabin and asked for the house of an old friend of mine. The young man
20 less warm - and stood in front of the fire to drink it. She asked: 'Have you come to see your Uncle Sam?' I had not, bu
21 r votes alone decide who is going to be mayor here.' When I asked her how many children she would really have liked, if
22 ading in her tired voice, but just as she was leaving, they asked her how tall she was. 'So I said, five foot two, and
23 ought to have handed the beastly things to the teacher and asked her if she wanted them, but they had been out in full
24 her to night school and wait to accompany her home. He had asked her to correct his English. Her English was a source
25 t it the madder I got. So I called Sabine at the office and asked her to lunch. We met at the Bottminger Schloss, a sma
26 g part in an interviewing panel for a new dance teacher. 'I asked her what method of assessment she proposed to use in
27 to pry some information out of her about my predicament, I asked her why the delay was so long. She didn't know all th
28 eny the source from whence that powder came. When the judge asked him how he first obtained it, he said that one night,
29 the language that Miss Lenaut had grown suspicious and had asked him if his parents spoke French. 'Jordache,' she said
30 mined. He felt the pockets of Liebermann's hanging coat and asked him to open his briefcase. Liebermann sighed but unst
31 s for long periods over several days. After a week, someone asked him what he wanted. The driver then started up the ca
32 ipal of a large boys' school said to me not long ago when I asked him what sort of boys he had, 'The sort that goes out
33 that I couldn't just sit in this man's office forever. So I asked him what to do. I mean, what I should do. He told me
34 you got her back, didn't you? Come, let's have a drink.' I asked him whether he wanted to be executed sitting or stand
35 the 9th Division who called himself the Entertainer. When I asked him why he said, ' 'Cause I rock and I roll,' and fli
36 . 'Why?' said John. 'Why am I teaching?' as if he had never asked himself such a question before. 'For the money,' said
37 l the very last moment of his trial. Was it conceivable, he asked himself, that Meehan was right? Had they in fact all
38 seemed incongruous wlth his hard-edged features. The Judge asked his occupation. 'Security consultant,' he replied. Th
39 ows up actively concerned with the Northern Ireland issue.' Asked how he became interested in politics he replied, 'I w
40 cut his throat are unworthy, and even unfounded. It may be asked how King could have been brought down in this fashion

asked

```
 1  you. I think I might know somebody ...' As he was going, I asked : 'How long would it take to get a certificate ?' 'Oh
 2  ials. 'I don't know why I'm ringing,- she said'chirpily. He asked how she was and what she'd done. She lied a bit about
 3  imself. 'Yes? What is it?' Hunt sounded impatient. Woodward asked Hunt why his name and phone number were in the addres
 4  David. He stared at her. 'Is something wrong, David?' Kitty asked. 'I have never seen you dressed up. You look very bea
 5   were pitching a large tent. They looked approachable, so I asked if I could stay with them. They were pleased to offer
 6  the men, one by one, left the room and returned. Then I was asked if I would like to wash, and I, too, walked down the
 7  , using the name Lewis. He paid for the room on arrival and asked if there were any messages for him; there were none.
 8  e was there, and he returned to the flat very depressed. He asked Irene to ring Betty and say the reporters hadn't show
 9  n cost-renting. Therefore, the first question which must be asked is how the total debt load in the owner-occupied sect
10  ety, English society. I like American society.' 'Do you,' I asked, 'know many people in American society?' 'Not really,
11  , you never told me you played the piano.' 'Well, you never asked me.' For a while she sat playing fragments, a few bar
12   mine—it even had the same kind of carpet on the floor. She asked me if I would like tea, or some sherry. I asked for s
13  s, it didn't look like him'. This seemed to satisfy him. He asked me one more question: 'Why does he seem to feel that
14  n, it reads: Until midnight I scarcely saw Harold, who then asked me to dance, and then we went up to the second floor
15  erally. People find fault with it. A drunken lady last week asked me what the hell my problem was. She said I was a com
16  lved it. After some more discussion of this kind, Uncle Sam asked me whether I had any friends, and I told him about Je
17   Now there's an interesting question,' he said. 'If you had asked me why I married Eva in the first place I'd have some
18  statement accounting for his movements over the weekend. He asked Meehan when he could come to the police station and M
19  ph said. 'You're not hiding anything from me, are you?' she asked. 'No. Why would I do that?' 'I would like to see him
20  urried away. I said to Captain Imrie: 'Sorry, I should have asked permission.' 'That's all right, Doctor.' We were back
21  re. Put it on for me, Alan, please.' When I had done as she asked she said, 'I'm sorry I was so silly last night, darli
22   far away, in Africa or Southeast Asia; but why, it was now asked, should not the same principle apply to the nations o
23   daffodils.' 'Sir, please what is a daffodil?' one bold boy asked. So the teacher drew one on the board, because none o
24  he efficiency of the nurses and how much they cost. Stanley asked Sylvia politely how Paul was getting on at school. 'O
25  e. Only recently it has been revealed that the Pentagon has asked that all the major hospitals in the US should keep a
26   and protective love. That I do know. It was she who always asked that her sister should come and make her home with he
27  rgent requirement. Had it occurred to the foreign editor, I asked, that I had only that very morning got back from Indi
28  an more?  One man, noticing the distress of a white friend, asked the cause and was told he had just lost his wife. He
29  e close friends, or stayed at their houses ever; and seldom asked them back to ours. Unless forced by adult politeness.
30  I was on the way to a local junior school, where I had been asked to chat to the kids before they began lessons for the
31  ith him. I stood up and looked at my watch which I had been asked to remove and place on the desk behind me. I had been
32  m just to stay the night.' 'No.' 'Well, your wife did?' 'He asked to stay.' 'Did you see him in the morning?' 'Yes.' 'A
33  roused herself from her daze, fixed her eyes on her son and asked, 'What are you going to write, Benny?' 'Stories of li
34  , but wanted to see inside a pub, where she had never been. Asked what she would drink, she said 'whisky', which she ha
35  very good job of the bathroom,' she said. 'Really?' 'And he asked what the marks were on the stair carpet.' Harris frow
36  en he took the phone, instead of talking to Clay Dillon, he asked where Walt was — Walt being Dillon's boss and the Cha
37  laining that my passport had been stolen two days before, I asked whether I could board the plane without it. Trying to
38  r said, ringing the extension. A man answered the phone. He asked who was calling, and Woodward identified himself as a
39  at happened after my daughter was born. The bank called and asked why was I suddenly signing my checks Mrs. Philip Hend
40  or him.' 'I don't know if my wife would agree.' 'Tell her I asked you to. I leave it to her - if it's too painful ...'
```

ask, asking

1 im to see who it was. Then, unexpectedly, the man laughed. 'Ask a stupid question,' he said, 'and get a stupid answer.
2 at a time.' 'And how much did you give to our baby, might I ask?' 'Ah,' he said, 'that's the whole point. That's where
3 uarantine and onto this uncontaminated island. Why, you may ask, are the French such dazzling lovers? And indeed, so yo
4 d the driver. 'Sure? Course I'm sure,' yelled the foreman. 'Ask Barney.' The other workman, evidently Barney, nodded. '
5 ssage standing beyond the moat below. 'Well, you did rather ask for it, Alan, didn't you? People who cosh people must e
6 . Go to her. Only please don't bring her here, that's all I ask.' 'Gertrude, you're killing me, you're mad, there isn't
7 ontact me - yes, I will. Just what I want.' 'Did you, may I ask, get any results?' 'Plenty of results,' said Mrs Oliver
8 y to me at home, after all. Does Mihal understand it, may I ask?' 'He likes to think he does. And that puts him in a go
9 ou want to know why he's a walking encyclopedia, you go and ask him yourself.' Sergeant Yates went out and returned fiv
10 hey are overcrowded and in deplorable condition. Why do you ask?' 'I don't know. Just say I've got an intuition that so
11 sense of the words? Or was he having me on? I don't like to ask in case he wasn't. And to add to my burdens, Josh said
12 g to speak to me, and turned my back, praying she would not ask 'Is anything the matter?' 'Is there anything I can do?'
13 hy word,' he said. 'It's a perfectly filthy act too, if you ask me,' said Wilt. 'Well, I must say it all sounds pretty
14 f the vote. 'I think there shouldn't be an election. If you ask me, the President should have a seven-year-term and, bo
15 s nineteen.' 'Never mind his size, how we find him?' 'Don't ask me.' We walked round to the bow. Somewhere ahead of us
16 robably Plato's 'harmony of the eternal spheres' (but don't ask me which page of his). And, except on Sirius or Aldebar
17 before a stunt, I always put my left shoe on first.? Don't ask me why - I just have to do it.' Performing stunts takes
18 I've no doubt, no doubt, it will - come to me. That's all I ask. Remember I'm there. The rest will be taken care of.' (
19 and she answered the vicar's questions breathlessly. 'May I ask something?' she said. 'Where is the nearest station?' '
20 ass for president, and that is the plain truth. Who else, I ask you, but Jefferson would turn the American army over to
21 or a month of Sundays. Sticking knives in people's backs. I ask you!' she exclaimed to the sky. 'He had a very nasty ev
22 n't go.' 'You want to come or don't you?' ' Yes, but let me ask you something first. I've just had a bit of an idea.' '
23 'Desiree! What are you doing here?' she exclaimed. 'I might ask you the same question,' I snapped back in my best Perry
24
25 ffer. An hour on the bus with a long walk at either end was asking a lot. It's a sign of how desperately she needed to
26 aiting to be done. I saw X in the X recently and they were asking about you and send their best wishes. They said
27 mi. But I am not leaving until I know your plans.' 'You are asking for a bullet through your brain.' 'You shut up, Nahu
28 sise to use this kind of gear in these conditions is simply asking for trouble. A spinning rod, fixed-spool reel and 10
29 don't worry. If they stopped us on the road, they would be asking for trouble, wouldn't they?' He smiled. 'We shall ho
30 ere are several hundred, but there is, at least, no harm in asking. Human beings have never been deterred from question
31 t to know it, for God's sake.' 'Don't get angry. I was just asking.' 'I'm not angry. I just said you ought to know the
32 g fiction; he knew it was not true. But Miss Bloomfield was asking me to believe that Uncle Nick had been insane all th
33 wer that.' Captain Burke retorted: 'I'm not asking you, I'm asking Mr Woods.' Kingsley: 'He's my client and I'm entitle
34 your plans, Kitty?' ' She laughed sardonically. 'I was just asking myself the same thing, along with a dozen other ques
35 oes that mean?' 'They're not lovers, if that's what you're asking. Neither of them is interested in sex with anybody,
36 warrant 'Must' rating there is but one escape. 'I know it's asking the world but what chances are there of the Black Pi
37 d. 'What the hell has that got to do with you?' 'I was only asking.' 'Well, just keep your nose out of my business!' Sh
38 for their trouble,' I said, angry with her now. 'I was only asking you a straight question and I thought I might get a
39 .' 'I'll never get over it,' she said, affronted. 'No one's asking you,' he said, and then he rose and pulled her up by
40 It's incredibly important, Atheliah, or I wouldn't dream of asking you. I can't really explain it to you over the phone

thought

1 ademoiselle Rouselle extended her hand. About fifty, Poirot thought. A fairly imperious woman. Would have her way. Inte
2 in the sky.' He put his fingers to his moustache to find, I thought, a lost bone from the fish. 'Young Bert Taylor admi
3 myself. I accepted the invitation. Inviting Franklin was, I thought, a sign of their willingness to open up to Marxist
4 . God, what a mess it all was! Sally clutched her knife and thought about Gaskell and what he had said about divorce. P
5 ng after his appointment, I imagine, he must have sometimes thought about the time when he was one of the people, the h
6 s up with laughter. 'Sorry he ever raised 'em, and so on. I thought all that stuff disappeared thirty years ago, but it
7 hed the furthest borders of her enemies. 'It's hopeless!' I thought. 'An absurdity. Why doesn't he come home?' And then
8   down and back into the sea. Oh my God, oh my God, help me, thought Anne. She thought, I have got to chance it, and now
9 ess and he hit him so many times. I always thought - when I thought anything about it - that it was just a man earning
10 became aware of another detail. The sky was not, as he had thought at first glance, completely empty. Dotted overhead,
11 om throughout the Bay Area, all gathered under one roof. I thought back on all the difficulties we had confronted tryi
12 favourite dark blue worsted suit and knitted tie. Damn it, thought Breslow, perhaps he would go with Kleiber across to
13 know what kind of an operation it was?' 'Lower abdomen, he thought. But he's not sure'. He leaned over to me and I not
14 , comical history of the ordinary bloke.' 'I shouldn't have thought Charlie Chaplin was very ordinary,' Zoe said, 'and
15 eight of her power, the number was 176. What was it now? He thought five thousand. Yes. What did that show? He replied
16 ance could continue only for another six months. After all, thought Guy, the young fellow must learn to stand on his ow
17 layer or labourer. She noticed him particularly because she thought he looked guilty, and mentioned him to her aunt. Th
18 e again but for a different reason. For an awful moment she thought he was going to ask her for the money. But he chang
19 ack for her, once he'd put his instruments in the car. She thought he'd hidden in the Gents and she waited behind one
20 magnificent house in the country, her dogs, her rabbits. I thought her nice but rather childish. Vita at that age was
21 that made me uncomfortable because I always admired him and thought him the person I should have wanted to be like if I
22 n account in an English newspaper of his success I suddenly thought how effective and interesting it might be for me to
23 e, nor did they, and she looked at the satin-wood table and thought how long it would be before they would grow tired o
24 tacked or something like that. And then I thought I saw - I thought I could see - an extended arm, among the brambles.
25 ght was lousy . . .' He didn't even wait for breakfast, she thought. 'I didn't say anything,' she said. 'You don't have
26 er. Not a word. Ok?' The door opens. 'What are you up to? I thought I heard talking.' 'Who would I be talking to, godda
27 hind Rose Hill's soft, still face. 'She's nobody's fool,' I thought. I longed for it all like an acid drink at the end
28 with my father without working under him. So I said that I thought I might enjoy some job involving 'figures'; and in
29 ou're full up just now,' he told her apologetically, 'but I thought I might just look round, with the idea of staying s
30 ced a definite twinkle in his eye at the suggestion, and he thought I was a most fortunate woman, as Eddie was a respec
31 ning to come through the hall, not unnaturally asked what I thought I was doing; and at this I jumped up, laughing at t
32 he fact that your mother doesn't love you?' For a moment, I thought I was going to hit him. Instead, I went through one
33 s of the times he used to have here. That was why I came. I thought I would be able to live my own life, and I thought
34 ou are, dear ' said Daisy. 'Now we see you, now we don't. I thought I'd got rid of you. I am just starting to celebrate
35 ched his free hand and waggled its first two fingers. 'So I thought I'd see if his father knew where he was or anything
36 ng out of school when I was a boy! Where are you going?' 'I thought I'd take them down to the wood to see if there are
37 the moment. We've been very busy, as you know, and I really thought - I'm sure you'll agree - that it was more importan
38 d at the Munch print of the scared girls on the bridge. She thought I've got to kiss him, it's the end point of the wor
39 sts, grinding their own axes. Many people, who wanted to be thought independent, also came to identify the future of th
40 disappointment and rage, as though dark had descended. She thought irritably, oh let it go, it's only Blesford Grammar

thought

1. also, getting the word and the symptoms. And then again she thought it could not be true. Perhaps it was the sun, or th
2. connected with - meths drinkers, prison reform, he vaguely thought it might be something of this kind - and yes, that
3. almost never was. The Victorians, like earlier generations, thought it more important to keep kitchen smells out of the
4. ing on the grey rough linen of her pillow. I would not have thought it possible that I could ever feel such deep pity f
5. there was a man waiting for Christopher and me. At first I thought it was the police raiding the magazine, it was alwa
6. ult part. She looked at the box, but hesitated; perhaps she thought it would spoil her dinner. 'Now, in my case', she s
7. Davis.' 'He didn't die of drink.' 'But I thought ...' ' You thought like all the others did. And you're wrong. If it's
8. ' 'I have something to do,' Rudolph said. Here it comes, he thought. 'May I enquire what it is?' Boylan poured himself
9. d sat down at the table, sobbing. He has saved my life, she thought, my beautiful son has saved my life. She tore up th
10. egetable or chemical odor. Female make-up is conventionally thought of as a means of disguising age and imperfections.
11. famous architect in England. But as a young man people had thought of him only as a mathematician and an astronomer wh
12. shelf was now spread open on the shelf. For a moment Thomas thought of locking up, but then he thought, hell, if there'
13. sted by rats and that the children played with the rats and thought of them as pet animals, something of the order of s
14. d have been home by now. Something has happened to him, she thought. Oh please, God, not him. She heard the door open d
15. ou make of it? They had a good case, you know. Very fair, I thought, really very fair.' Mr Mawne straightened his shoul
16. ligent and she's suffering from shock, though I should have thought she could have found a better man in her extensive
17. ert and fluffy. Anne was about to refuse the drink but then thought she had better accept it. 'Thanks.' Daisy gave her
18. later her friend Joy rang to tell us she'd seen Debbie and thought she was now 'on the streets'. That evening Hil and
19. ctors the ratio shoots up to 300: 1. Westergaard and Resler thought that a ratio of 13: 1 indicated inheritance with a
20. any people don't bother, and the law is not enforced. It is thought that about a million puppies are born each year, ab
21. oulder wearily uphill over and over and over again. Tolstoy thought that life is all very well as long as you are intox
22. could not possibly have said. It was more likely, she later thought, that she had been weeping for the knowledge that K
23. go on to minerals. Our fathers had to drink to be men. They thought the beer made them strong and fit. But this is wron
24. up again when she had finished. Lucy stared at herself. She thought, The girl's a genius. Even Tusker said, 'Good God!
25. , or Rousseau, but we hardly think of Aristotle, whom Lutfi thought 'the most penetrating mind ever created by God', as
26. k-out' on Christmas Eve. We wanted to choose a time when we thought the Security Police would be drinking and off guard
27. contacts with his former colleagues. Bernstein asked if he thought there was any possibility that the President's camp
28. eally been doing and shipped him to Siberia.' 'I would have thought they would have shot him out of hand.' 'They would
29. ing, 'Look at her.' Hugh stared at his wife angrily and she thought, 'To hell with him. Can't I even look at another ma
30. went the joke on the other side of the Avon, R. J. O. Meyer thought to liven up morale by buying a piano for the Somers
31. noticed I was being watched by the mother and the family. I thought to myself, 'Now I know what it's like when the cows
32. a was crying. The doctor had just left, and he said that he thought Uncle Sam might not have more than a few days - or
33. nto classes. Until then everybody had to accept what Auntie thought was good for them, nourishing wholesome food, if so
34. he hand with a stick. When asked by the magistrate what she thought was the cause of this sudden assault and abuse, she
35. young, dark-haired girl was waiting to audition too, and I thought, well it's her, she'll get it, of course.' Campbell
36. The fact remained, however, that she was gone. At first he thought, Well she has got herself lost and is wandering abo
37. nd could not explain. Lying there at his side in the sea, I thought, 'What is the matter with Andy, that he cannot see
38. stability.' 'Besides, Philip will be coming back soon.' 'I thought you said he wasn't?' 'Oh, that won't last. He'll be
39. line. 'Grace says you told her to come over here. Why?' 'I thought - ' 'You think he's dead, don't you? You think he d
40. might go to your head Or do you want to come and dance?' 'I thought you'd never ask,' she said, as they went off. Dan s

think

1 y anything except 'yellow' about one hundred times. I can't think what it meant.' 'He is dreaming of beautiful blonde g
2 tribal divisions. 'Have you got a ruler?' 'A ruler? I don't think I've got a ruler. Do I sell rulers?' he asked the gir
3 any of this stuff?' the girl asked. 'Well, not yet, I don't think.' 'What's the matter? Aren't you feeling so good?' 'N
4 ke a sledgehammer to her.' In the corner Dr Cox fainted. 'I think I'll have another whisky if you don't mind,' said Pro
5 f you ever need any rope, don't hesitate,' he says. 'God, I think I've got about five times what I need here.' 'Not yet
6 t. 'There's some brandy in the dining-room, Mrs. Leonard. I think Mrs. Taylor would like a drink.' I sat down in a chai
7 mother said. Something she heard. She heard it in Malaya, I think. Gossip there from other people. You know how they ge
8 yes - of course,' he heard himself stammering. ' Er - oh, I think a gin-and-tonic - large gin, please - ' ' Slice of le
9 just the opposite of Charles - ' ' But that's the point, I think.' 'What is? I don't see what you mean.' 'It's not eas
10 n to land at Vinh Long, where the pilot yawned and said, 'I think I'll go to bed early tonight and see if I can wake up
11 ege! I did not rise to this bait. 'To be frank,' I said, 'I think Hilary Jackson has always been a silly girl, but she
12 fore they'll give it to you.' 'I've got that,' she said. 'I think.' 'I'd rather you didn't handle it, if you don't mind
13 had flight insurance been less readily available. Those, I think, are Vernon's arguments - and the ALPA's.' Mel glance
14 , because my deadline was 1.30 p.m. Rather early, you might think, for the American news that would be read over tomorr
15 ke him?' said Marcus. 'Calverley General Hospital, I should think,' said Daniel. 'It's got a psychiatric ward.' 'Is it
16 ut china. He'll forget all about the punchbowl! ' 'I should think that's a foregone conclusion. But I'm glad you like t
17 'No,' I answered, 'but it would be the best thing, I should think. She'll be looked after properly, if it's the aunt I'
18 . 'That's one of the things everyone's got against me, they think I'm mad to live in such a place, but I like it, I rea
19 owe. 'And what will he say to this enterprise?' 'I dread to think. He's not keen on verse drama.' 'Or on me,' said Crow
20 from error - -a demand never made of professional writers. Think of all the notes of acknowledgment you have read at t
21 o have a look at the crater as well.' 'God almighty, do you think we're on a bloody holiday jaunt?' There's some steep
22 a moment she says, 'What's happened to your friends, do you think?' 'They're all dead.' Patrick slows down a little. Sh
23 ing him out of your sight.' 'When will you be going, do you think?' Lady Frances said. 'As soon as possible,' Adam repl
24 face and naval in language, met him. 'What the hell do you think you're doing, Laugmuir, messing about with the bloody
25 unity for hours and hours of chat. I said, 'How long do you think the rain will go on?' 'Who knows? It's very unusual.
26 to school affairs. 'Should you phone to the office, do you think, dear? It closes at five, you know, and if you need a
27 edition did you use? Do you still meditate? I say, do you think we could have a talk some time? No one here is intere
28 owler's niece who works at 'The Bell'.' 'Is is true, do you think?' I asked. Miss Clare lowered her knitting and looked
29 ve his head. He put his hands above his head. 'Where do you think you're going, son?' the guard asked. 'I'm visiting Mi
30 Who, and my father, but what do you think I am? Why do you think I've changed in my life? Do you think I suddenly read
31 sees one, old Gaspard,' Willie said comfortably. 'Don't you think you ought to talk to him and tell him he'd better lea
32 d shouted. 'There's plenty more on the ground! ' 'Don't you think we ought to get out while the going's good?' ' No,' h
33 'A flight to Rome! An airport is so interesting, don't you think, especially for a young, intelligent person like you?
34 g the company, when Ellen came into the kitchen. 'Don't you think you'd better slow down?' she said. 'I'm fine,' he sai
35 estruction. I agree with you there, Anna.' 'Mike, don't you think I'm right?' Anna turned to the tall, watchful actor o
36 'She's my wife, actually,' I said. 'Rather nice, don't you think?' I hadn't the heart to wait for a reply. Mrs Rossite
37 is head. And he died.' 'That's awful,' she said. 'Don't you think I know that?' I answered, getting testy. 'Easy, Frank
38 Desland. The crying sounded so - well, upsetting, don't you think?' 'Yes, I admit that. All the same, I dare say just h
39 de pocket of his jacket. He looked at his watch. 'Don't you think we'd better be going?' They walked three abreast towa
40 e us. 'Didn't they get any warning?' 'I don't know.' 'You'd think there'd be a warning.' 'Maybe there was.' We walk to

according to, apparently, allegedly, to quote, in the words of

1 antee created 'significant legal and political problems,' according to a bank memorandum. Richard D Hill, the bank
2 Britain's 600,000 diabetics to reduce their insulin intake, according to a book published today. Dr James W. Anderson, a
3 r position within the family is tell-tale. Second children, according to Adler, try to outdo the first. The third child
4 ght and one other. The board was electrically operated and, according to a sign it carried, made in Italy. It was a mode
5 y the two girls I picked up?' The Police started searching. According to Betty they searched everywhere, in the cupboard
6 k was most hospitable with his bottle of Johnny Walker and, according to Dick, the pair parted expressing great friendsh
7 g down, urban people are fleeing from the cities. 'Nobody.' according to Dr Mansholt, 'can afford the luxury of not acti
8 to these marshes at 4 am, up to his knees in water 'with', according to his diary 'an east wind blowing strong and rain
9 s will have quite another resonance at a funeral or picnic. According to Irving Goffman, the concept of 'proper dress' i
10 peasant in the Tuscan hills above Florance. His early life, according to legend, was spent tending his father's flock. T
11 at the studio. Jimmy Roland, who sometimes helped him, was (according to Piglet) in Paris. Tim tried sometimes to sell t
12 tly two hundred years before I myself set foot in Serendip. According to the Oxford English Dictionary, Walpole told one
13 sed. Studies at both Wye College and at Reading University, according to Wibberley, 'give no support to the suggestion t
14 at is not the case.' 'It is not the case? When you had made according to you three long-distance telephone calls to Stra
15
16 aves arethreadlike and aromatic. Height up to 5 '. There is apparently an old Welsh saying that: 'He who sees fennel and
17 e. We're supposed to discuss some text I've assigned. This, apparently, can be anything that comes into my head, except
18 sat down and lapsed into an unhappy silence. Castle said, 'Apparently Davis is ill. I was in late this morning. He's ch
19 tried cats, it was said, but that hadn't worked: the cats, apparently, didn't love her back. But one thing was indisput
20 would be next to die). Jefferson gave us news of Hamilton. 'Apparently he became sick a few nights ago, after dinner wit
21 just moved here from the Middle West. She's got the money, apparently. Inherited brewery money. Old German family. But
22 least about - is what to look for when buying a double bed. Apparently most women make three big mistakes when buying th
23 hole building would be ready by January 1963, though Utzon, apparently, never agreed these dates. This first contract wa
24 's a Mobile Murder Headquarters,' Peter Fenwick explained. 'Apparently some maniac has buried a woman at the bottom of o
25
26 l go on trial at Grimsby Crown Court, Humberside, today for allegedly assaulting a man causing him actual bodily harm a
27 st three papers have gone ahead and published their stories allegedly exposing the players' private lives in New Zealand
28 d Philip that the building was being checked out for a bomb allegedly planted during the night. The search, he understoo
29 partment, was among sixteen people arrested on Saturday for allegedly stealing bricks from the demolition site on Buchan
30 time to come. Vendors are often reluctant to take back such allegedly unsatisfactory goods unless the customer can produ
31
32 e apparently knew by prior notice, would be a non-event. To quote his words: 'The battle is lost before the first shot i
33 lmut Jahn, Frank Lloyd Wright and Mies van der Rohe. But to quote Mailer again, Chicago is a city where 'nobody could ev
34 convinced her way is the only way.' Says one opponent: 'To quote Proust, she has the single-mindedness of the second-ra
35 kingly moralistic book about a corner of New York where, to quote the British publishers, 'nothing matters except the pr
36
37 isruptions of the natural ecology, we may literally, in the words of biologist Barry Commoner, be 'destroying this plane
38 Caspar Weinberger that the risk was 'low, very low,' in the words of one. 'I could not say he questioned the assessment
39 United States, and MacArthur proved to us all that, in the words of that old song, 'Old soldiers never die, they just f
40 age only made it more difficult. Yet it was, in Gaitskell's words 'a very unusual by-election'. The two-week Bristol cam

add, begin, continue, go on, interrupt, mention

1. e a picture in a gallery. 'You're very nice. Although,' she adds, 'another time you should try having wine for lunch ins
2. ce Minister) is 'perceived as being in trouble', the report adds. His top aides are worried. Furthermore, Mr Foot, ' for
3. ly, the most efficient police force in Europe. And, I might add, in case you have any illusions about the Swiss, that ou
4. e girl didn't tell her that he was her father! We laughed,' added Mrs Oliver. 'Yes, we laughed a good deal.' 'Well, tell
5. s you?' 'She likes us both the same,' she says quickly, and adds, 'She says that, anyway.' Sometimes the fit of unhappin
6. I'd be in for a very unpleasant surprise one day. She also added that he had a great deal to worry him. He had. After e
7. t and they revolt when they're hauled into action.' Or, she adds, they may be snobs, unwilling to associate with ordinar
8.
9. he do so, do you suppose?' 'Mihal would like him to,' Amur began, but Ranji interrupted: 'Taba will not let Mihal have
10. nching them apologised. 'I hope you started without me,' he began. Clint paused. 'Yes, we've been doing some talking. Do
11. s. Or at least Simonius got down to business. 'I think,' he began, 'that I should, perhaps, explain the problem as it wa
12. hty pounding. He has had a thought about his book. The book begins: 'The attempt to privatize life, to suppose that it i
13. he roared out his merriment. 'Perhaps we'd better leave - ' began the vicar timidly, just as I was saying: 'Annuals in a
14. and heading off for dinner. 'Got a bit of a problem, boyo,' began Thomas. 'Hoped you might be able to help.' 'Well . . .
15.
16. or whatever this lunacy was - passed. In a quiet voice, he continued, 'As usual with me, the world saw fit to believe t
17. amiliar with his book.' 'You must read it,' Sabine's father continued. 'But since you have not yet been able to do so, l
18. to,' he then said. I did want to. 'Unfortunately,' Simonius continued, 'I must spend the rest of the day at court. So I
19. e sipped her beer again. 'Haven't seen much of you lately,' continued John Franklyn, raising his own drink, 'What's up?'
20. s countenance flashed into my mind uncomfortably. 'Anyway,' continued Miss Clare, 'the child went off very happily this
21.
22. l day stand ing on their heads.' He laughed grimly but then went on 'And why not, why not? They are right. If you're poo
23. ight be interested, but all she said was 'Oh.' 'Because,' I went on, cutting through a crust, 'because our father won't
24. hey assesed him very favourably. 'The second applicant,' he went on, 'is a little older and has had experience in infant
25. bury Investment Trust was interested. 'However,' the letter went on, 'it is perfectly clear that with so few of your sha
26. ea, but she had gently declined. 'There's a spare bedroom,' went on Mrs Annett earnestly, 'and we truthfully would love
27. emain unsolved, it should fall on me.' It was difficult, he went on, to imagine what else the police could do. He cited
28.
29. ing to delight us by trying on the queen's gift—' 'No, no,' interrupted Cal. 'It wouldn't delight you the least bit, my
30. me maniac ...' 'Come now, give credit where credit is due,' interrupted Dr Board. 'There was obviously an element of pre
31. e saw me. I said that I was sorry about the quarrel, but he interrupted me : `No lad, I don't want you to say you're sor
32. which started up inside their chests. 'You mean,' Francois interrupted, 'that your heart starts beating faster?' 'No, F
33. gaping Boon, 'And this is -' 'I recognize Mr Boon, dear,' I interrupted. 'We were at the same party a few weeks ago. I d
34.
35. in his highly authoritative History of the Church, actually mentions having seen this statue, a two-figure work comprisi
36. lded arms, trickling diamonds over his sleeve, and casually mentioned: 'I thought I had something of interest for you, b
37. man. They say she was originally a barmaid but that's never mentioned. Most of the time she lives quietly in this damn g
38. he thought. 'Miss Graham,' she said slowly, 'Mrs. Berkeley mentioned that David was fatherless. She didn't tell me - fo
39. and phoned me at the office to tell me. Then my mother had mentioned that she would be out the following evening—she wa
40. ms to have more than a little truth in it. It is also worth mentioning that the criminal world does not seem to be very

admit

1. They weren't admitting anything, or, at least, if they were admitting anything to themselves they weren't saying it out
2. scorn. 'I like making pictures of course,' Ford reluctantly admits, 'but it's no use asking me to talk about art.' Ander
3. pretend nothing had happened. A piquant incident, you must admit - but wait till I tell you the sequel. Howard Ringbaum
4. e world as 'son of Oliva and Pepita', a statement which was admitted by both sides to be untrue. All the others were des
5. people may well struggle on for months, even years, before admitting defeat. But again the people who lose, and the peo
6. ernment.' This programme, if carried out, will, Livingstone admits, double the rates. What brand of socialist is he? 'Fi
7. ed. 'Things have not gone quite as smoothly as we'd hoped,' admitted Dr Bottger. He was a scholarly-looking man, sixty y
8. good teacher. He grunted. 'I don't remember your name,' he admitted. 'Elise Trotter.' She dipped her smeared eyelids. O
9. be not going his way, is now a much more positive bloke. He admits going through a spell when he was content to sit on h
10. I was pregnant. She told me about her pregnancies. She even admitted having doubts about being a good mother! ' As she a
11. ficient heater, and the temperature inside was low. Yet, he admitted, he had been nervous. It had been a test he had had
12. top it. The fact that he had not only done so, but publicly admitted himself to be in the wrong, had impressed Ash a gre
13. t how wrong the Government were. He at least is prepared to admit his mistakes. Others are not.' The parliamentary strug
14. Well what would you do instead?' I thought about this, then admitted : 'I don't know'. 'Quite. Neither do I. We've got t
15. d I usually talk to each other. This isn't communication. I admit I'm upset, you are quite right, and there may be an el
16. of the winter to see how he makes out as leader of what he admits is 'not the greatest side to have left these hallowed
17. listic version of Rhoda Courtney. Although he couldn't have admitted it, he was proud of the painting: it was so translu
18. the boy, or that she had any previous knowledge of him. She admitted meeting him on the day of the hare-hunt, but said s
19. ke a governess, though I don't know much about them, I must admit.' 'Oh, have I?' Though the tone of this question illus
20. vast army of poachers is operating with almost no control,' admits one conservation official. In the Russian federation
21. , in fact, that it even unnerved the judges. Penny Vincenzi admits relief that she was a judge and not a competitor, con
22. sue despite the writ and the publication of Jimmie's letter admitting 'responsibility' (which, as he might have expected
23. . They went to the museums and art galleries which Gertrude admitted she scarcely knew. The idea of simply visiting thes
24. by his death. A-a-h. How romantic. Mind you, Teresa Stangl admits she was terrible angry when her husband volunteered t
25. rain was missing, he questioned my grandfather. Grandfather admitted taking it, saying he had no choice. The next day th
26. satisfaction. Anne still could not like Tim, but she had to admit that it looked like a case of two people in love. They
27. not till The Day.' I asked when that would be, and Jackson admitted that no exact date had been set. 'Mr. Breen's handl
28. ; that although they were guarding them they didn't want to admit that the prisoners existed. The first soldier to have
29. 'It was the hardest thing I ever did in my life,' the nurse admits. The doctors refused the sisters as donors, on the gr
30. doning his side? See what I mean?' ' Can't say that I do,' admitted the Lieutenant uneasily. 'After all, it's not as th
31. h other. It helps to clear the air if a parent occasionally admits to a child how angry she or he felt - especially if t
32. ould pay grotesque sums for paintings he sometimes secretly admitted to be amongst his worst. On one occasion Rhoda rema
33. n, for her, is merely an opportunity to pamper herself. She admits to being difficult to live with: she is probably too
34. oughts. The Rosses had been attacked by two men. Meehan now admitted to being with another man. The Rosses had been atta
35. r than Walt, or Ken, Boney Harris or even the curate. And I admitted to her, in a loud, rough voice, that she was even p
36. ask at his desk towards the rear end of the room, he had to admit to himself that Miss Lenaut might be beautiful, and un
37. s pink and white good looks, and seems much younger than he admits to. His voice is clear and light like an army chaplai
38. utable about both his features and his personality. He once admitted to me: 'I don't think anyone really knows me - not
39. nald what his position would be if, during his evidence, he admitted to the crime. Mr McDonald said that as he was now a
40. Jimmie was his stepfather, although that fact had not been admitted within or without the family for many years, not, i

advice, announcement, assurance, claim, comment, information

1. what was being done to provide relief. She repeated urgent advice that all people outside the disaster area should stay
2. wo Dollars', repeated. Five weeks later, in spite of Lee's advice that the visit should be delayed, Washington ordered
3. g used as re-motivators. An obvious instance is the classic advice to a young secretary: 'The more typing errors you hav
4. Tusker shouted one day. Exasperated and ignoring Ibrahim's advice to do nothing until Mr Bhoolabhoy was back from his m
5. esult of sitting around all day doing nothing. The doctor's advice to her was to 'get a job.' (If you were awaiting tria
6. is a severe hang-up somewhere, but Mr Crackling rejects my advice to see a psychiatrist. I have rarely encountered such
7. xture which may bring a blemish to them.' He continues with advice to the woman on how best to coax the good out of her
8.
9. ght, and Boon's continuing monologue, are interrupted by an announcement from the captain that they will be landing in a
10. or the by-election at Croydon, North-West, are expecting an announcement later this week that October 22 has been chose
11. save face, the company isn't saying it's lost. The official announcement that the strike was over was ambiguously worded
12. at on the plane for a while after landing and then came the announcement that we should go to the transit lounge while t
13.
14. days later. And that I will be able to give you an absolute assurance about the status of our cruise missile project aft
15. mined to get a conviction. The Crown Office may have had an assurance from Mr Struthers that the guilty men were Griffit
16. Such demands would in the present day include the absolute assurance of full employment, a constantly rising standard o
17. n East-West talks. He said he wanted to give the clearest assurance that he set the greatest store on carrying out his
18. his point to my solicitor, and only when I had his absolute assurance that the other person would not be called to give
19. ned to the desk and tapped ash into a tray. 'Do I have your assurance,' the colonel asked, 'that you won't do anything a
20.
21. ts with the president of the United States, despite all his claims of friendship with the director of the FBI, an obscur
22. is issue. Few, though, would go along with the Commission's claims that commercial forestry and wildlife conservation ar
23. rial fishing pressures. The sea is getting dirtier. Despite claims that our rivers and coastal waters are on the mend, a
24. ence will show that the claim of political persecution, the claim that the defendant is a political prisoner, the claim
25. here boggled in reverse. I can accept, that is, Pasadena's claim to be 1,000,000,000 miles from Saturn, even though lac
26. e pundits seek to pull on us is that we should accept their claims to 'excellence' because these are expressed in terms
27. s I also believed implicitly. It was obvious to me that his claim to know more than any man in the world was justified;
28.
29. tair's ear infection. Only after several days of occasional comments about 'my head hurting' did we begin to wonder seri
30. s all most heartening. Mrs Pringle, to whom I made a blithe comment about the fine weather, did her best to turn the wor
31. at is going on and may be up to a bit of it himself. To his comment 'I thought Joe Bloggs was in Australia,' you should
32. y. We noticed him leaving, but thought it better to pass no comment. Instead I'd visit his house to talk things over. Tw
33. I skimmed through the columns to see whether there was any comment on my contribution, and sure enough there it is: 'Tu
34. herself in rows over productions, apart from the invariable comment that it was all costing too much. She liked coming o
35. ied approval. Aldous Huxley, for instance, made the caustic comment that 'since the Fall, total innocence has been ident
36.
37. was impressed that Kitty came from America and relayed the information that he once owned a photograph of Mrs. Roosevel
38. inally, a senior officer came to me with the cheque and the information that I owed just over sixty pounds. In her prese
39. 7th and the Police Gazette of July 15th. Both contained the information that Mr Ross had heard the intruders call each o
40. and the sergeant clearly thought it was Valium. I added the information that the pills I took were for depression, and t

advise

1   ough one would be unwise to visit it. I certainly would not advise a first visit on a day of uniform greyness, or of wet
2   s of the Churches' Unity Commission. Last year's conference advised a 'positive response'. But I guess it is a sign of t
3   roperty, the money to invest?' 'Yes, I knew that.' 'Did you advise against it?' 'I was in Washington.' 'But your propert
4   se babies who are still waking for 2 a.m. feedings, I would advise against letting them sleep through the 10 or 11 p.m.
5   any hospital or clinic. We do not prescribe. We do not even advise. All we want you to do is to talk, and talk guardedly
6   es because the same company makes both . . . The Commission advised an immediate reduction in recommended retail prices
7   ied and a waste of time that might be put to better use. He advised Ash to abandon any thought of marriage for at least
8   heir control. Many people suffering from osteoarthritis are advised by their doctors to lose weight, because any excess
9   rking as an assistant in the shop, selling bait and tackle, advising customers on what to buy, and helping with stock or
10 mal delivery. If the doctor foresees complications, he will advise going to hospital. The woman who has her baby at home
11 bly this would include a description of the car, and Meehan advised Griffiths to get rid of it at once. (At this time of
12 rnals addressed to what used to be called 'the career girl' advised her how to dress to attract 'the right kind of man'
13   to tell her what had happened, and I guessed that they had advised her not to mention anything which might upset me aga
14 ged Metternich had been advising the new young emperor, and advising him never to make war. But the emperor had made war
15   remainder of the cake. 'You should taste one of those,' he advised. 'I get them from a little baker in Glendale. Maybe
16 or the manager, go back and point him out.' Miss Kelly also advises: 'If a woman can see that she's going to be left alo
17 ses were brought to the Director of Public Prosecutions. He advised in one case that proceedings should not be brought a
18 t so fussy with an older child. Most doctors nowadays don't advise keeping children in bed unless they feel ill enough t
19 ny room at home, have you?' 'No. Though my security officer advised me to.' 'I don't suppose you'd tell me if you had.ye
20 ys Barbara. 'That's right,' says Howard, 'I will.' 'Can you advise me when?' 'Well, I'm teaching this morning,' says How
21   voice. 'I'm visiting Israel briefly on business. Could you advise me whether to stay a few more days, or - ' 'The only
22 of 61 called Thomas Haxton, said he didn't know himself and advised Meehan to ring the main office when it opened; and o
23 rtaking it well before final year.   Careers staff can also advise on the importance of obtaining vacation experience in
24   In every campaign in which I have been engaged I have been advised 'Open your columns to the opposition.' My reply has
25 nce against him, particularly in the absence of a lawyer to advise Parker what to answer and what not to answer. Nor wou
26 ys that even doctors are not doing as much as they could to advise patients not to smoke. He claims that when doctors ex
27 longer, browner. 'Ladies don't cross their legs,' Miss Keep advised. Rhoda seemed to prefer her father, though he didn't
28 'd rather not.' A friend of mine who has been married twice advises, 'Shrug off the little things that irritate you and
29 s of depression and nervous troubles. It was his doctor who advised that he change his job towards the end of that eight
30 that at the moment there is nothing we can do; we have been advised that it would be pointless to appeal. I suppose we h
31   I was menaced by a bear? Fire your gun into the air, I was advised - that's usually enough to scare them off. 'But I ha
32 ind is another possibility. Although in 1733 Alexander Pope advised that 'the proper study of mankind is Man', psycholog
33 ook out a single one hundred dollar bill. When possible, he advised Thomas, he should always try to have a hundred dolla
34 ad takes much longer to deal with. You are somehow cheerily advised to 'spread the load and banish washday '. This seems
35 uld be arranged. Miss Clare, with true village caution, had advised us against going to Mrs Moffat too precipitately. 'L
36 rbed him, and was on the run again. His companion left him, advising Viktor there was only one place to go - the Foreign
37 ttending pupil visited the principal by appointment and was advised which classes to attend. Now, on the first day of ea
38 old Woodward anything that was incorrect. It was he who had advised Woodward on June 19 that Howard Hunt was definitely
39   the service you need any branch manager will be pleased to advise you and set the right wheels in motion. (' If you wan
40 ow - gift or faculty or something. Now, listen - I strongly advise you to let it alone. Don't ever try to do anything yo

answer, reply

1. t over-valued, and who was the most under-valued artist: he answered 'Andrew Wyeth' to both questions. Wyeth is very pop
2. sh the mud off his jodhpurs. He was steadfastly refusing to answer Andy's questions about where, or if, he was hurt, and
3. e candidates are welcomed. The Admissions Tutor is happy to answer any queries from individuals or schools, and welcomes
4. e said mechanically, 'What are you going to do?' She didn't answer. 'Aren't you going to write about it?' ' Write about
5. ke had an ironic quality. For example, one man said that he answered at least one advertisement a day looking for work.
6. Then someone said, 'What do you think?' 'I don't know,' he answered. 'But what do you think?' He paused for a long time
7. y financial. You swear and I lose a pupil.' My question was answered by a lad of fourteen. 'Neill is talking rot,' he sa
8. ied. 'How did they manage to persuade her?' 'They didn't,' answered Dr Martin smugly. 'I did!' The car moved slowly for
9. o and bury my father, and then I will come back.'' The king answered, 'Go and bury your father, as you promised you woul
10. look awful. Are you all right?' I couldn't move my lips to answer her. 'Ginny?-' she said with alarm in her voice. She
11. years older. 'Where the hell are you going?' he asked. She answered him coldly, 'To see my father out in Long Beach. He
12. d no to him. And he doesn't get his hearing back until they answer him with a yes. Well, he has heard my no many times.
13. ria. 'There's never an occasion for it.' He couldn't resist answering: 'I should have thought you might wear it on your
14. ial. 'And was that nice?' Flick was saying. 'Well, it was,' answered Karin, 'but I wish I'd known Alan then. I'd have go
15. o smart?' I asked. 'I wouldn't go for coffee with you,' she answered. 'Listen - I wouldn't ask you.' 'That,' she replied
16. of a lawyer to advise Parker what to answer and what not to answer. Nor would Dr Robey testify in court as to what he ha
17. ew. We then reviewed the questions, all of which were to be answered simply 'yes' or 'no'. ls my name Philip Burlington
18. old us to bring him here, so that you could see him, and we answered that the boy could not leave his father; if he did
19. e asked whether they have done their exercises they usually answer that they haven't had time or have forgotten all abou
20. that we should overthrow the government of Florence, but I answered that your state had never offended me and that I wa
21. ed by the concealed, contradictory 'But'. No matter what is answered to the last 'but', this person will agree 'yes' and
22. on asked: 'How can you tell when he's lying?', and promptly answered: 'When his lips are moving'; sometimes on the spotl
23. ot know that on the Sunday?' A guilty man would surely have answered with a monosyllabic 'No', and left it at that. Meeh
24. eling of 'togetherness' fostered in the meeting? If you've answered yes to some of these questions then your committee
25. ry. 'Why can't I call my mother if I want to?' 'Because,' I answered, 'your mother is dead.' In the gay town of San Fra
26.
27. essor Cohen, how do I know that I exist?' The keen old prof replied, 'And who is asking?'. I directed this against mysel
28. long since forgotten the days of the week. 'Good morning,' replied Bowman. 'How's it going?' Poole helped himself to co
29. laces and said, 'I walked through the rain.' Still I didn't reply. He let the shirt go and looked away to the flooded st
30. heard a woman remark: 'But I adore his paintings.' A second replied: 'I adore him! He's always been one of my heart-thro
31. f she was!' I did. But not for long. 'Look, Mrs Pringle,' I replied, 'I think you're all makng far too much of Margaret
32. eople asked Gericault if he had not painted it, to which he replied: 'I wish I had.' Two years later in 1824 Delacroix p
33. comment 'I thought Joe Bloggs was in Australia,' you should reply 'Oh dear, it's that silly girl. She's typed the wrong
34. e play, and I was asked if I would be interested to which I replied that I had not even read it yet. I was going down to
35. ature we will be able to avoid it in future. The pessimists reply that the virus which caused the fever is still at larg
36. ights to Rome.' As if a button had boen pressed, Miss Young replied that Trans America had direct non-stop flights from
37. hy may not women travel so? It is unfair!' 'Well, my dear,' replied the colonel in a tone of some amusement, 'you have o
38. e to reply; it is regarded as bad manners in Britain not to reply to an invitation. If you are not sure what it is you a
39. here only a short time.' I was intrigued. 'I research,' he replied to my question. 'My family, we lose many records in
40. . Y'all take care now!' This last simply meant 'Cheerio'. I replied with the conventional 'You too' and, putting my hand

apologize, nag, quarrel, scold, tell off

1 ad eaten the meal in ominous silence she thought it best to apologize again for her lateness and did so speedily, before
2   his hat, made a little bow, and handed her his card. 'I do apologize for bothering you,' he said and then he waited, wa
3 e. He considered dropping in, giving her the opportunity to apologize for having been rude; possibly telling her that he
4 he will also appreciate the contrast and can often be heard apologizing for 'losing his head'. Some individuals take sup
5 olina.' Sam kissed Carolina's hand with some grace. My wife apologized for not being able to speak English which is to s
6 d with what seemed a pound of bacon crumbled in it. Abraham apologized for there being only a quart of milk for everyone
7 of his bigger one. 'Sorry I haven't called you yet,' Beynon apologized; 'I was in and out of Linz all last week.' He sat
8   her pretty, fluttering smile. 'My husband', she started to apologize, 'must return to Greece by flying boat yesterday n
9 s reach, my sister and I decided to let him in. He began by apologizing profusely about what had happened, explaining th
10 vernor. He had the job, which he obviously did not like, of apologizing to me for what had happened, and I listened with
11 eed not more than a week after her terrible accusations she apologized to Michael for what she had said and assured Kay
12 n't believe what was happening around me. I was continually apologizing to the Chinese about our behavior. One member of
13
14 d her faults but they were just reflexes. She couldn't help nagging and criticizing any more than you can help saying it
15 ay with him for week-ends. Once I even allowed myself to be nagged into inviting him for a day or two to my parents' hou
16 rents, I couldn't stop. My boy friend used to tell me, 'You nag me just like your mother nags your father.' It frightene
17 . 'Why don't you ever make cakes, like other mothers?' once nagged my son, who hates cakes. A doctor once told me to do
18 we hear ourselves telling our husband not to drive so fast, nagging our children to clean up their rooms, and we know al
19 their orange squash, so that I could rinse out the cups, or nagging them about putting the rubbish back into the picnic
20 financial situation, and only wrote after being nagged and nagged to do so by my husband. He had tried to sort out my f
21
22 t me to do what he wanted, I did everything not to. We even quarrelled about who should fetch the Coca Cola. Perhaps bec
23 d tonight. I spat on her. She made me spit on her.' 'People quarrel. After three years a thing doesn't just end like thi
24 tion. I seldom looked my mother in the eye in those days. I quarrelled bitterly with my sister, ignored my brother. Abou
25 ack in Glasgow events took a curious turn. Martin and Darky quarrelled over money: Darky shot and wounded Martin, who wa
26 rances Dickinson, with whose husband the elder Robinson had quarrelled over the sale of a cow. Mary Spencer also complai
27 t he had spent years like this, begging for half-crowns and quarrelling with landlords about foreign coins in the gas me
28
29 l of two. 'It's the two of us against the world. Mother may scold but no one loves you more.' It is her defense against
30 enerations of parents and schoolrooms-full of teachers have scolded children for eating between meals. Although children
31 eading was about. There is always someone who recalls being scolded for 'guessing' instead of 'sounding out' the letters
32 ed and cross. But when we have to go in, we have to.' Don't scold her; it won't make her see the error of her ways. Don'
33 ted out. Quickly but silently she darted out of the cell. I scolded myself for having said yes in the first place to her
34 th us?' Aurelia suggested. 'Don't be silly, Aurelia,' Milly scolded. 'You're all acting like Daniel's never been out of
35
36 r' she indicated the absent policewoman with her head - 'to tell me off for not ringing the police. I know my husband, h
37 old. 'Someone was always my favourite at one time. If I was told off by my parents I could come along to the kitchen. Th
38 of a sense of humour. Imagine spending your early mornings telling people off because they had not got their second she
39 always be a man, anyway. All the senior mistress does is to tell the girls off for wearing the wrong colour blouse or so
40 onfidence? And when we were confident, about the play, they told us off for being big-headed. So it all started with tha

1 d management has also benefited from lower labour turnover.	As a recent study suggested, 'job enrichment, under the cov
2 and name, asserting status through Conspicuous Consumption.	As a teenager once explained to me, 'Adidas are the best T-
3 been quietly petrifying for several million; but Teitleman,	as Agrot had indicated, was certainly doing his best. An un
4 e this far. But this was not the end of Raes's discoveries.	As already mentioned, he had two samples of reasonable size
5 r than a man of exactly the same weight to propel her body.	As already stated, women have traditionally been confined t
6 g effect. During the second half of the nineteenth century,	as Anne Hollander has pointed out, there were two sorts of
7 rstood how delicate was the political balance at its start.	As Arup himself admits, '. . . it was explained to me that
8 rness or good manners, derived from an expensive education.	As Bernard Shaw once said, 'Do not do unto others as you wo
9 Site of Special Scientific Interest every single day. Yet,	as Chris Rose demonstrates in Chapter 3, landowners and the
10 her with all her children, but especially with George, who,	as Dot said, 'had an unfortunate habit of nicking cars'. Ge
11 position to give or receive compensation. And in any case,	as E. Mishan has shown, the outcome will depend on the rul
12 an combine equal parts of evaporated milk and boiled water.	As explained in the previous paragraph, the bottle needs on
13 e long been available in Japanese cars. That's no accident.	As GM chairman Roger Smith told us, 'If you're going to des
14 hese rules and habits and values have become worldwide, and	as Golding and Elliot argue, 'news changes very little when
15 he great transition of horse by machine and the years when,	as Gregory put it, 'nothing was bought and nothing was sold
16 life of repentance - or rather, what a life it isn't! But	(as he'd written in one of his weekly letters) the only way
17 nts that eventually prevented Charles Darwin from becoming,	as his father predicted, 'an idle sporting man'. Darwin was
18 uire a much more elaborate change in our society; and thus,	as I argued in Chapter IV,1 we cannot see clearly how to ac
19 er direction. 'You don't have to work this afternoon?' 'No.	As I told you, the Treasure is closed on Tuesday.' 'What do
20 ector Flint was not to be drawn. The notion was too awful.	'As I was saying,' he continued, 'what we need now is hard e
21 dent. The changes that have taken place in Cambridge House,	as I've already indicated, were closely connected to the ch
22 dges who share his general political and social views. But,	as I've mentioned before, a President is sometimes deceived
23 nlightened; and a gradual increase in equality will itself,	as is argued in Chapter VIII, still further diminish the in
24 esday night group? Are there things that should be changed?	As Jill, a tutor, put it: 'We're a bit worried that we're t
25 only when men and state are one that man achieves liberty.	As Kedourie noted, 'in this new theory freedom is, even mor
26 t of that episode. His friend was obviously impressed. And,	as Mary recorded in her notes: 'If anything could convince
27 ad often went unpaid, gave Drew, Gould and Fisk a bad name.	As noted, they are still referred to in the history books a
28 potential aggressor very unpromising. It has the advantage,	as Roberts points out, of being organized along more purely
29 m what she had been as a girl before her marriage. In fact,	as she had once confessed to Judy, sometimes she thought sh
30 and over, 'to get a bit of clean air into the poor things,'	as she so tactfully told me. ' That leg any better?'he enqu
31 ,000 passengers by 1990) could be met in a variety of ways,	as shown in Table 6. All assumed that Heathrow would be dev
32 ect to the historical and geographical vagaries of fashion,	as Sir Kenneth Clark has demonstrated in The Nude. In twent
33 hen compared with the structure in the U.S.A., for example.	As someone remarked, 'the rich get richer, the poor get chi
34 way, you see a constant stream of advertising images which,	as Sontag has suggested, appear almost more real than reali
35 f children, especially little girls; less respectable ones,	as Stephen Marcus informs us in The Other Victorians, went
36 irrefutable. Unfortunately it is also extremely simplistic,	as the author himself admits. It fails to acknowledge the s
37 tuated with individual effort or hard work. But since then,	as the last chapter pointed out, there has been a growing t
38 as been written about the results produced by good parents.	As Tolstoy wrote in Anna Karenina, 'Happy families have no
39 there is almost always an associated decline in birth rate.	As two Stanford researchers have stated: 'From a broad look
40 together.' 'I can't say they've done that. I am interested,	as you may have heard, in special branches of my profession

bark, growl, grunt, roar, snarl, snort, whine

1   son, it's about the flag.' His face turned dark red and he barked abruptly: 'What flag?' Terry and I exchanged lightnin
2   ike his in the audience. In the schoolroom, the teacher who barks at his pupils to 'sit up straight' is demanding, by ri
3   the unscheduled or the unexpected. ' Ridiculous!' he would bark at Mother as she sat composing drafts of her epitaph. '
4   rdana sprang to her feet. 'No!' she said. 'Sit down!' Kitty barked. 'It's nonsense, I am behaving shamefully.' 'You are
5   t you'd say that,' Gretchen said. 'Company, about face,' he barked out. He made a smart military turn, clicking his heel
6
7   tting words. I was 'smart'. 'What have you got there?' he'd growl at me, when I was reading a book. 'Ah, Mr Smart?' Befo
8   heir new schools at the end of this term. 'Sorry I'm late,' growled Dr Curtis. 'My brother's staying with me and wanted
9   decided to so inform Maud. Staring stonily at Willicombe he growled 'My dear chap, there's a bit of a war going on here
10 lay jokes. I came abreast of him; he spat, glared, and then growled out, ' 'Ere, mister—what is that supposed to be ?' s
11 ll have no objection if I ask you to.' 'None at all,' Laing growled, 'you want me to resign?' The prime minister flapped
12
13 too listless, too dazed and too bewildered to do more than grunt a 'yes' or 'no' to my few queries, but it was enough t
14 n the neck-band of his collarless shirt. 'Nearly seven,' he grunted. 'Better get a move on, miss. It s choir practice to
15 mmat for her, Doctor, do!' 'I am doing all I can, my girl,' grunted Dr. Chilgrove. 'Do you fetch Mrs. Strudwick and tell
16 ork,' says daughter. 'Ssh ... this is a good TV programme,' grunts father.) Over the Malacca straits in Indonesia, and y
17 mpts to excite him with the proposal I had come to make, he grunted 'Uh-huh' and 'Uh-un' between, or during, mouthfuls.
18
19 s, until in the end he stopped putting me off tactfully and roared at me over the phone, 'She doesn't want you! Isn't th
20 urrent problems would have been nonexistent. Finally he had roared, 'Ginny, this is ridiculous! Get up out of that bed t
21 tarted to turn on the detective, his face red with fury. He roared out, 'Goddamn it, I said lock him up.' Michael, still
22   to erect a steel road block. 'What do you mean, he's out?' roared Valentin to the weeping wife of a taxi-driver in Egle
23 hole, a breach. He charged in. 'But this is in English!' he roared. 'What does it mean in English? Nothing! Idiot! You h
24
25 ise, the black-haired youth grabbed her arm, shook her, and snarled : 'Are you going to shut up?' I now noticed that a s
26 r bordering on lunacy. 'We've been made to look idiots,' he snarled at Sergeant Yates. 'You saw them laughing. You heard
27 d I smiled slightly in recognition. 'I'm all right,' Rodney snarled, ' but you're gonna have to pay for my machine to be
28 und the corner he caught my arm. 'Marnie!' 'Let me alone' I snarled. 'Don't you know what I mean when I say, no? Leave m
29 er ...' 'For heaven's sake, do you have to go on about it?' snarled Dr Mayfield, but Dr Board was not to be stopped. 'Qu
30
31 xi out of New Palace Yard. 'They didn't know who I was,' he snorted. 'And who were you?' Churchill inquired. Or rather h
32 apable of dealing with the contingencies of life. 'Oh,' she snorted, 'cats! There are too many of them.' But because he
33   her ideas, but she's getting a trial, isn't she?' The girl snorted it was a frame-up and went off in search of a true b
34 rch suspected only too well what the other might be up to), snorted 'Oh, all dolled up, are we?' and then let her pale e
35   'Try and get it out of the way by tomorrow.' 'Pack-drill,' snorted Thomas when he reached the office. Although the shor
36
37 thetic.' Two little boys were treading hard on their heels, whining for money: 'Memsahib!' they appealed. 'Memsahib!' a
38 low. As I opened my front door he tried to come in with me, whining: 'I'm so hungry - so hungry,' and grinning vacantly
39 og-eared. I held out my hand. 'I have no money left,' McFee whined. 'It is all spent.' 'That is too bad,' I said in repl
40 'But the kite will be lost! Some other child will find it!' whined Patty. 'It is not far—I believe I saw it come down ju

be

1 equest upon request to the administration, demanding that I be placed in some more normal section of the jail. She went
2 ved to be correct. From the outset, we had insisted that it be a joint venture but the school understood this to be doi
3 of survival. He went to Mundek with the proposition that he be allowed to take up the job of courier through the sewers
4 ee. The United States attorney George Hay then asked that I be committed over to a grand jury on a charge of misdemeano
5 d to keep Bouvier's copy. His only request had been that he be allowed to seek the cooperation, in confidence, of the h
6 of the Republican National Committee and suggested that he be contacted. Broder described the official as a 'very stra
7 mouth. Apparently the gateman, having insisted that the box be opened, prodded the animal dubiously and said it didn't
8 filed a motion with a San Francisco judge requesting that I be recognized as George's legal investigator - which was es
9 ld the court, he had gone to Jefferson and suggested that I be given a foreign embassy to remove me from the scene. Thi
10 wspaper tales of Geronimo's evil deeds, recommended that he be hanged. The advice of men who knew better prevailed, and
11 ribune Group meeting on 3 September, he demanded that there be either a general election or a referendum before I Janua
12 e was attacked by the Conservatives who demanded his salary be cut. The Conservatives were seeking to exploit the publi
13 eaving them overnight, the prime minister ordered that they be taken to women's prisons That would shame mothers out of
14 otball while I was working. I proposed that indoor football be forbidden. I was supported by some of the girls, by some
15 Meetings; and on one occasion, she carried a motion that I be put out of the school on the ground that I was useless.
16 n's ability to stir up the people. So Marshall ruled that I be tried in Ohio for the misdemeanour of trying to levy war
17 this surplus. (The Old Testament carefully urges that they be treated well; for instance, it forbids the farmer to yo
18 nservation advocates have frequently advised that buildings be better insulated; they also point out that most industri
19 well-ordered society. Jackson insisted that a public dinner be given me at Nashville, complete with parade, music, spee
20 okshops which dominate the town) and decreed that passports be issued. 'Dukedoms were offered for sale, in the manner o
21 -year-old, had brought his friend home and demanded that he be taken in. Tom Hagen was given a hot dish of spaghetti wi
22 ranch house Chivington stopped and ordered that the rancher be hauled out of bed and taken as a guide. This was Robert
23 of Philosophy said, Oh, yes, the Chairman had asked that he be registered in an Ideas and Methods course which the Chai
24 skance at Paracelsus, the City Council could insist that he be allowed to teach. The Frobenius family was printing book
25 v's immediate personal life has initiated a request that he be medically helped. There is no history of mental illness
26 rank of major-general. President Adams then proposed that I be promoted to brigadier-general, but Washington turned me
27 ed merely to depress her. Why did Dr. Vogel insist that she be here? It wasn't as though she were dying. Miss Sturgill
28 miliar with the subject, and suggested that Henry Kissinger be invited to come over from Georgetown and sit in on the m
29 re of teeth. It is sometimes recommended that babies' teeth be brushed when they have their first set of molars. For mo
30 not trusting my self-control. I had requested that no cards be sent in. I wanted to ignore Christmas if I could. We wer
31 to Florida, as a prisoner, he asked that after two years he be allowed to return to the reservation. Crook thought the
32 security adviser, Mr Zbigniew Brzezinski, suggested that it be called by its name. The United States, he said, echoing
33 ng my freedom, but they would go on record demanding that I be released pending the determination of my innocence - or
34 igorenko's mental health and firmly recommended that he not be hospitalized for further examination; the Serbsky psychi
35 mething like, 'Her family requested that the cause of death be kept private, and since there was obviously no crime inv
36 rstand Imran's anger when England recommended that the ball be examined, for he is a tremendous polisher of the ball. T
37 e mail which poured into my office at UCLA demanding that I be expelled from the university. He knew about the many thr
38 ined up for inspection. He also ordered that sailors should be trained to say 'left' and 'right' rather than saying 'po
39 ity with Brother Wilt. Peter Braintree proposed that a fund be set up to help Wilt with his legal fees. Dr Lomax, Head
40 liament considered the matter, and advised that legislation be introduced to allow reluctant peers to disclaim their en

believe

1 statesman. Adoring women treated him like a man of genius, believed all that he told them, typed his manuscripts, gave
2 himself, was always left to the Security Police - or so he believed. And in his case, after all, there could be no fear
3 the translation. I have told you about his scruples which I believe are a curse from his old mother. My husband', she co
4 have him release a transcript of White House tapes that he believes are related to the Watergate inquiry. The transcrip
5 tly. 'A poet's first study is himself.' Miss Musson, Scylla believed, felt some concern over Cal and what would become o
6 quite easily to me now, even though I secretly and guiltily believed him to be right. This range-war mentality had been
7 d rolled slowly down her wasted cheeks; the fact that Ashok believed himself to be her son had been so sweet to her that
8 ger worth my place as a bowler. By the end of the summer, I believe I had done much to answer both charges. Certainly, t
9 Freneau's newspaper, but then he had the fortunate gift of believing implicitly anything he himself said at the moment
10 was one I couldn't believe in, Hurtle.' 'I'm surprised you believe in any of my paintings. Doesn't it go against your '
11 ery exact specificity, since our chemist friends? Ford had believed in discouraging students from night work, since the
12 an I feel the same way? I've given up on my family, I don't believe in marrying and having children, but I think there's
13 sensible preliminary but Eva was a sound sleeper and didn't believe in pills of any sort. 'I can't imagine why not,' Wil
14 mantic story, your marriage, isn't it? The lady's German, I believe, isn't she, or Danish; and you were married recently
15 an an incessant attack on the government for the wrongs she believed it had committed against the people. All Bolshevik
16 address to denounce education in general, and the things he believed it led to in particular. There is no doubt that we
17 o you thinking of opening the glass phial ? ' 'My superiors believe it might be very dangerous to do that. Dr. Rothstein
18 which he had not yet done. Byrne had seemed pleased. He too believed it was something of a coincidence. Hurriedly, Alexi
19 he people in Marin County, who were both white and wealthy, believed me guilty of kidnapping, murder and conspiracy. But
20 Duke Ellington kissed him on both cheeks - the last time, I believe, Mr Nixon was ever kissed in public, except by next
21 livered before, had annoyed him in more ways than he'd have believed possible. Bertrand's girl was looking at him interr
22 e thought well of in terms of what they have read. Teachers believe that a boy or girl who willingly reads history books
23 ther with an exaggerated hug which she barely returned. She believed that any emotions openly expressed must be false em
24 t it. D. said she was like Iago, and that nobody would ever believe that such a person could exist. M. said she reminded
25 , exposing the raw flesh. I saw that I had been mistaken in believing that Uncle Nick was mad. He was neither more nor l
26 an position on the Rio Protocol. Because not many Peruvians believed the documents to be genuine, the Lima station had g
27 s that although following the maths quite well the students believed the pipe to be a solid bar. Regardless of my descri
28 apabilities. A test does more harm than good if the teacher believes the result tells her what the child will always be
29 cing evidence that cancer is caused by stress, as is widely believed. The very idea that rich Western countries have the
30 cize what it's really like for girls on the street.' Eileen believes 'the women themselves must do the talking or it's n
31 the second half of the 1970s, the International Socialists believe themselves to be hovering on the brink of a major br
32 ht of itself. The founding fathers of the American Republic believed themselves to be the inheritors of the civilization
33 tics. 'Do you know any palindromes in French?' 'No. I don't believe there are any palindromes in French. It has somethin
34 on this issue shows the difficulties of maintaining what I believe to be a false distinction. At one point, Willis and
35 say, a school-teacher in horn-rimmed spectacles and what he believed to be Druidic robes. The crown was awarded for, as
36 k about the militant feminists in America, whom the Chinese believed to be good soldiers and organizers. When we told th
37 righten, his wife, who was pregnant, and was doing what she believed to be right. He was truly sorry for Marcus. He miss
38 he commanded. They hesitated, not believing - or wanting to believe - what they had heard. 'Now!' he shouted. Slowly and
39 And she was then quite normal?' 'She was always neurotic, I believe -' 'Where was she at the time of the suicide? Was sh
40 ed my Swiss counsel. ' Well, we seem to have reached what I believe you call 'the point of no return'. They are no doubt

claim

1 in, despair, ecstasy - and recovery! St. Dennis was, Alexis claimed, a genius in his poetry, his art, but a genius, as w
2 ter it was finished, ignoring her letters and telegrams (he claimed afterwards never to have got them: which may have be
3   twenty-nine minutes. A certain distinguished Boston banker claims an even faster time, but when one is discussing sub t
4 er design; the result is Wren Gothic, and St. Mary has been claimed as the 'earliest true Gothic Revival church in Londo
5 ing a glimpse of the past. 'The !Kung are a good model,' he claims, 'because, compared with prehistoric hunters and gath
6 ccommodation would be a blow to London's tourist trade, and claimed Board of Trade support for the view. Philip Unwin, o
7 s of problem-solving in complex situations. Both, Hirschman claimed, can act as crutches to the uncertain decision-maker
8   there ail their lives. Some two dozen Thaxted families can claim continuous residence in the town for several hundred y
9 whim bring the wine in a jug and it was even better than he claimed, dark purple and as powerful as a brandy. Fabrizzio
10 n her distant prime speeds in excess of 160 m.p.h. had been claimed for her, but at this moment I was running-in a set o
11 re is no conclusive evidence that it does any of the things claimed for it; yet for a time it caused teachers to think a
12 a questing, driven, thought-dominated man of the West, they claim. He is a total being, whose mere persistence in being
13 velling, some witnesses said later, at 60 miles an hour. He claimed he was driving at 50, in a 30 mph zone. He crossed o
14 s or of increasing his inputs. Were he to decrease them, he claimed, he would have to lower his standard of living drast
15 d. Two evenings during the week and one day of the weekend, claims Hemphill, make you acceptably gracious. This would se
16 imagined them formless and torpid. 'It would explode,' she claimed hopefully. 'Now you are imagining it on an electrica
17 er of slick, minimalist boxes, Donald Judd, whose work, she claims, 'is a whole made of non-hierarchically related, rela
18 ys that it is 14, and the other who swears blind that Denis claims it to be 20. I can see four possibilities: Denis is p
19 istro bar and saw herself as being on stage. Allen Ginsberg claimed Liverpool was 'the centre of consciousness of the hu
20 or example, a study of airline pilots found that the pilots claimed not to feel anxious or worried (indeed most said the
21 ary, simply that this one has never met George, although he claims often to have seen him across the footlights. He is c
22 the truth was that Lionel had on several occasions legally claimed Pepita as his wife and five of her seven children as
23 der than the average Leaker imagines. He can often be heard claiming that 'anyone could act in the movies' or that 'dipl
24 xams sidetrack proper personality development. Only pedants claim that learning from books is education. Books are the l
25 ntroversy to the boil in the early part of this century. He claimed that Mars was covered with a spider's web of fine li
26 hat he had not been paid his wages. On the other hand, Dadu claimed that the boy had stolen a goat worth 120 rupees and
27 ing like a bee' had forced it into her mouth. Both children claimed that they saw mice constantly running up and down th
28 t the time of the children's growing up. But she could have claimed the right to freedom years before. Years before. Wha
29 andy had another name no one seemed to know what it was. He claimed to be a Scot but had a powerful Liverpool accent. He
30 cause Pauling is a distinguished chemist, although he never claimed to be an expert on virus diseases such as colds, his
31 ncerned, there was a greater proportion (40 out of 108) who claimed to be life- long non-smokers than among the men, but
32 ion, The Times and the Daily Mail daily published what they claimed to be the inside story of what was going on, slating
33 e truth ended almost immediately. Miss Haynes, it was said, claimed to be twenty-four and had been, on the best authorit
34 cicers might emerge from a room which someone had finished, claiming to have found dust on a skirting board, or outside
35 standing by the back wall. Brody assumed he was the one who claimed to have witnessed the accident. He was gazing absent
36 eleven homes, tearing up floors and furniture in what they claimed was a search for fire-bombs. The police action touch
37 sses. They found a bottle of methylated spirits, which they claimed was illegal liquor. Two African policemen took me to
38 in June is a predictor of voters' agendas in October', they claim. With television the impact was last minute, but immed
39 ing wealth. Many citizens grumble about this but few, Downs claims, would abolish bureaucracy if given the chance. ESCAL
40 ed-earth history of humankind, and triumphantly conclude by claiming, 'You can't change human nature.' This little catch

congratulate, bless, compliment, praise

1   as though he were a child. They looked each other over and congratulated each other on looking well and went into anot
2   Durham and a Conservative MP also spoke. Lambton was warmly congratulated for appearing on the same platform as a polit
3   d which would overflow everywhere into the street. Kate was congratulating herself that she had not, when she paid the
4   of his way to guide me through the red tape jungle. When I congratulated him on his efficiency, he told me that consid
5   luxurious office, he shook Lexington warmly by the hand and congratulated him upon his aunt's death. 'I suppose you kne
6   the more objective aspects, he could throw modesty away and congratulate himself on having achieved his intention as a
7   to the voices, breathed in the jumbled bouquet of perfumes, congratulated himself that he was not married and loved no
8   fe has given up trying to get me to give up is smoking.' He congratulated me on my appointment as editor of the Dispatc
9   eived me with, 'Well, you didn't get far, did you?' He then congratulated my escorts for their keenness and courage. We
10 ofar as we could help to make the world a better place. She congratulated the delegation for representing the American
11 an occasion that brings relatives and friends flocking, to congratulate the parents and to see the baby. This is grati
12 ctresses.' 'I see,' said Frederica. 'I'm sure you do. May I congratulate you again on your excellent performance, which
13
14 me to involve heavy spending for arms. This, we've seen, is blessed as sound while spending for welfare and the poor is
15 er that the justification for - ' Mary Stuart sneezed and I blessed her, twice, once for her health and once for the he
16 and laughed at their future idol Andrew Jackson. I at least blessed him for the friend he was. The grand jury was empan
17 the shop. There was an extended handshaking ceremony. Akim blessed Kitty and Karen and all their subsequent offspring.
18 ssed over two hundred thousand words. Many times that day I blessed my experience on the Cardiff Western Mail and the c
19 essed the dog, he blessed the open sky and the sun, he even blessed the canal. He crawled up the slope of stones until
20
21 the crowd by Court aides to chat with the Queen. 'Did you compliment her on her coolness in a tight situation?' was t
22 oticed at once and soon put a stop to it! The guests always complimented her on the flowers and she always accepted the
23 rate of production I shall be out of debt in four years.' I complimented him. I too have had my nail manufactories whic
24 o heavy bags, Willie is talking hard to the station master, complimenting him on having won second prize for growing th
25 s than ninety-two net. On presenting the prize, Lady Armory complimented him on his success in the face of wretched pla
26 terrupted only by much-applauded pregnancies. Then Hamilton complimented me for my part in the debate on the Judiciary
27 epted with suspicious gratitude. I could smell a rat. After complimenting me on my work, he informed me of a new financ
28 rieties of ice-cream; to being called 'Professor', to being complimented on his accent by anonymous telephonists, to be
29
30 a was that she was to do an article on him, because she had praised a play he had directed. At the luncheon she hadn't
31 rg in the mid-sixties provides us with an answer. Sylvester praised Bomberg's early work as 'standing out a mile from e
32 is rather bitter. Yet the American sub-species was actually praised by Scientific American: 'A salad plant equal to wak
33 e greatest orchestral master of all in our sense, is seldom praised for his instrumentation; his symphonies are too goo
34 damned. Over and over again I saw heroines forgiven - even praised - for the most dubious behaviour if they could clai
35 omething she could do, her high-school English teachers had praised her 'gift for expressing herself' so highly - Britt
36 professional friend in Italy; he had never met Haldane, but praised him for remaining within the British Cabinet as a p
37 eft. When Jim Callaghan stood up at a Labour conference and praised Mr Foot for the sacrifices he had made he was, in e
38 a strictly Russian characteristic but I doubt it. Reviewers praised the company for giving London 'the real Chekhov' bu
39 ly new one of unofficial disruptive strikes.' He went on to praise the courage of Barbara Castle: 'A commentator recent
40 a.m. and I had time to read the local morning paper, which praised us for the approach and style of our batting yester

criticize, blame, charge, condemn

1   mits. The government was allowing the Press wide freedom to criticize, and the establishment of independent political di
2   ht readily have become a planning disaster - and indeed was criticized as a potential disaster in the late 1960s. But in
3   to improve the Post Office's image were perhaps justifiably criticised as 'gimmickery', but unfairly dismissed as purely
4   ts to mark the big rooms on the first floor. The design was criticised at the time as 'insipid' but in fact the regular
5   they are welcome. But the playgroup movement has also been criticised because of its neglect of working-class areas. Pl
6   fraid to speak to neighbours in the lifts in case they were criticised for being unmarried mothers; some were so apprehe
7   40 per cent of the UK market. In Britain, the firm has been criticised for not making a wider range of electrical goods.
8   twenty-six last April and up to a year ago he was regularly criticised for what were interpreted as 'his attitudes'. 'Yo
9   7 from the Select Committee on Science and Technology which criticised its 'excessively timid' position on tidal energy
10 stoves by getting his fingers burnt ever so slightly. If I criticize my little daughter about trifles, you may say I ha
11 initely decline because he felt certain the honour would be criticised on the grounds of their personal friendship; he d
12 oke in public in defence of a general he considered wrongly criticised over the shell shortage. 'I have not come,' he to
13 ther than on genuine political debate.' The two geographers criticize the engineers for 'narrowness of approach' and a r
14 use of Lords had been totally avoided. Charles Pannell also criticised the proposals as no more than 'a little pruning m
15 innocent - made me laugh. My way of laughing has often been criticized. Well-disposed people are amused by it. Others ca
16
17 orry, Mrs Kirk, I really am,' says Anne Petty. 'You mustn't blame Anne,' says Howard, 'she has her own scene.' 'I'm not
18 ead from the borders of Turkey to the Rock of Gibraltar. He blamed 'British intervention' as the reason he had been unab
19 line in the quality of an ancient alliance. The French were blamed for everything; at one point, a temporary meat shorta
20 disapproving, children invent a wicked companion whom they blame for the naughty things they have done or would like to
21 o crime involved, I agreed,' but he wouldn't. I can't say I blame him.' 'So what did you do?' 'I tried to get hold of hi
22 p on time with the tickets instead of half an hour Iate and blaming it on the Tube when you could smell the booze on his
23 t day. If the baby has a fever after that, it should not be blamed on the inoculation; it is due to some new infection.
24 gets done. Of course, if there's an accident then it'll be blamed on the worker and the supervisor will plead ignorance
25 g sources: the playwright blames the director, the director blames the actors, the actor blames the director, the critic
26 no medical problems of any magnitude have yet been reliably blamed upon excessive fruit-eating! So, now that you've take
27
28 Lunchtime came and went, I ate what I could. I was formally charged by a policeman in my cell, with my solicitor present
29 n Torun where he lives with his wife and three children. He charges that perks, not progress, have become an obsession o
30 e denied that one could identify a roll of film. But when I charged him with theft, he was quite indignant and completel
31 . 'You can't do very much more,' said Wilt. 'You've already charged me with murder. What more do you want? You drag me i
32 icycles. Brought up before a General School Meeting, he was charged with 'constantly breaking the private property rule
33 William Macintyre said. He is very worried that he might be charged with receiving money from the Ayr crime. It was part
34
35 t is that one does know. Many people today are too ready to condemn a composer for 'not being able to hear what he has w
36 d it interesting. But Adler's theory and practice have been condemned as being superficial - the 'psychology of the trav
37 d in Chapter VII. Workers who take managerial posts are not condemned as traitors to their class. Trade Union leaders ar
38 reativity. Students who went along with his rules were then condemned for their inability to be creative or produce a pi
39 nt of English Literature at the University of Rummidge, has condemned the present sit-in by students in strong terms. 'T
40 to renounce his peerage and retain his courtesy title, and condemned the report as 'partial and inadequate', describing

demand

1 said. 'When was the last time you kissed a girl?' Mary Jane demanded. '1928,' the boy said. 'To celebrate the election o
2 n. . . how do you like that?' 'It's terrible, Mr Stein.' 'I demanded a blood test. I know the law. I demanded a blood te
3 nding with her legs apart in the middle of the room, loudly demanded, 'A drink someone, quick!' This display of energy a
4   often a child's eye is bigger than his stomach and he will demand a plateful that he cannot consume. To force a child t
5 hite became infuriated, called the plumber on the phone and demanded an explanation. The plumber would not back down. Wh
6 e stood in silence a moment. 'You here with anybody?' Islip demanded at last. 'No.' 'I see. Just out trying to scare up
7 n't resist it.' 'And what about his wife and children?' Tom demanded bitterly. 'I know you think he was selfish, but sur
8 tion movement. Posy was undaunted. 'What do they mean,' she demanded, 'by a 'population problem?' They mean that they ha
9   brilliantly white teeth. 'Why did I never see her before?' demanded Cameron. 'Oh, she and her brother were two dusty sk
10 as going with you,' cried Madge. ' To do what?' her husband demanded darkly. 'Not what's running in your head most of th
11 hiavelli patted her hand in kindness. 'Desperate situations demand desperate remedies.' She shrugged her shoulders despo
12 'sneerers', and the Left in the highbrow Press. 'What,' it demanded, 'do the any-country-but-my-own brigade argue? They
13 said. Her forefinger traced the line of her lower lip. Mary demanded, 'Is the money there?' 'Yes - it's there,' she said
14 to his dignity and the blow to his ambition. 'Why Aitken?' demanded Lord Derby. 'There are many Lancashire MP's with st
15 re look like hung round with a few bits of gilt cardboard?' demanded Mrs Pringle majestically. It seemed best to assume
16 hich were not jokes at all. What was the meaning of it? she demanded. 'Now, now, Mrs Green, what is there to get excited
17 to bowl her hoop. However she rapidly tired of the hoop and demanded of Jem the bootboy where he had put her kite—she mo
18 ed our dishes clean for us. 'What's happened to you?' Eddie demanded of Mona and Atheliah. 'You two used to be the most
19 g in the Tower of London, held on 16 June, Richard suddenly demanded of the assembled company what ought to be taken to
20 makeup. 'You fellows going to talk in here all night?' she demanded. 'Okay, okay, honey,' Thomas said. 'We were just co
21 e could pick them out all around us. 'See it? See it?' Betz demanded. 'See the reddish tint? My God, we've got grass in
22 use she wanted the experience of an election. Well?' Elaine demanded. She had sensed that Gareth knew this young woman.
23 concurrently telephoned McGovern. McGovern was furious and demanded that I call him. As we talked I could hear family s
24 her work; and more important, she is happy in it. One firm demanded that its employees should have at least passed the
25 s long overdue. The British were in an uproar. Most of them demanded that P. P. Malcolm be removed at once, General Char
26 re was an emergency in the building. Still not satisfied, I demanded that she explain further and finally got her to adm
27 , after the death of her first husband; her new husband had demanded that she leave the scheme and live off his eamings
28 can offer.' When the Bloemfontein control tower insistently demanded that the identities of all passengers should be dis
29 enegotiation. At a Tribune Group meeting on 3 September, he demanded that there be either a general election, or a refer
30 he said) and living with a married man, that his mother had demanded thirty thousand dollars from his father if he wante
31 aving behind her a counter piled with all the goods she had demanded to be displayed to her, a shop assistant awesomely
32 of love and fertility, once descended to the underworld and demanded to be let in, threatening to smash down the gate an
33 or routes suggested by opposing club secretaries, he would demand to be met with his team at the station, at, say, 9.15
34 opped him. 'I can just see my parents ! They'd turn up, and demand to be taken to the nearest gipsies. 'Take me to the g
35 zi, who knew no ltalian, rushed up to the steering room and demanded to know from the captain what it all meant, The cap
36 hang translated. I laughed. Her ancient eyes flashed as she demanded to know what I was laughing at. She was proud, curi
37 as stopped by two policemen disguised as human beings. They demanded to see my exemption papers. As always I showed them
38 iting at the gate. He stormed into the manager's office and demanded to speak to him. 'He's not here yet,' said the secr
39 sia.' Now Patterson glared at his audience. 'Convinced?' he demanded. Von Amsburg turned to Bosch and Schmidt. 'Gentleme
40 ad she hadn't when Marsha grabbed Jane by the shoulders and demanded, 'Why?' Jane stiffened and flared but Marsha didn't

describe, call, define, refer

1. n Murphy. Mr Harper started reading the papers with what he described as 'a certain amount of suspicion and cynicism' bu
2. ence books, announced that he was preparing what the advert described as 'A major motion picture with a budget of fiftee
3. y generations, such families could no longer conceivably be described as a ruling class. A few owners of country houses
4. was entirely within his rights. The interview, which Carlin described as 'a very lengthy interrogation', lasted an hour,
5. ing in the region. Tropical forests have with accuracy been described as 'deserts covered with trees'. ((2. Felling tre
6. took her seat in the witness box. Mrs. Marjorie Morgan, who described herself as the wife of a retired tractor shop owne
7. Bradlee on a Watergate story. The Wall Street journal once described him as looking like an international jewel thief.
8. s still alarmingly yellow. Tom listened sceptically as Pyle described how he had thrown a hand grenade into a cave and t
9. n' said Bierce. Hearst did not complain to Brisbane when he described McKinley as the most hated creature on the America
10. es he had managed to write and conceal from the doctors. He described them as 'my only weapon', i.e. as his only defence
11. t 5.00 he reappeared and, with a cer- tain amount of pride, described what he'd done that day: 'Brakes, rocker box, batt

13. mes be what the seed needs. I suppose I'm what people would call a coward.' The grocer didn't attempt to hide the distas
14. passed from parent to offspring by chemical units which we call 'genes'. Variation is largely due to a reshuffling of t
15. ch too?' he asked. Well, he doesn't know everything. 'Don't call her 'she,'' I said. 'Doesn't Jennifer teach?' he asked
16. seven years it has been their only home. It is what they'd call in Scotland a crofter's cottage: one door, one combinat
17. eat Russia, that is, or Muscovy, as our forefathers used to call it - are also famous for their vodkas, and rightly, but
18. like to do. The psychologists call it 'negativism'; parents call it 'that terrible No stage'. But stop and think what wo
19. up stories to produce his own kind of writing. What adults call scribbling is the beginning of composing, just as babbl
20. only son of a wealthy Greek shipowner. 'I suppose you would call us wealthy,' he told me. 'As a boy I lived in Wembley;
21. raditional associations are with slums (by 1598, Stow could call Wapping 'a continual street or filthy passage'), the Lo

23. cklash occurred, and I felt the need to relax. Someone once defined a crank as an enthusiast without a sense of humor, a
24. hools' there were 61 life-long non-smokers. (The scientists defined a non-smoker as anybody who had not smoked as much a
25. ort of structure to work to initially. Fridays were loosely defined as a day to 'get to know Bristol' By lunchtime on Mo
26. ren and young Persons Act in 1933, the term 'girl-child' is defined as 'a girl who is over eight but under fourteen year
27. Or 'intellect'? Turn to page 3493 where 'to understand' is defined as being 'to apprehend the meaning or import of', 't
28. ever, isn't she?' The art of dealing with children might be defined as knowing what not to say. On the other hand, it i
29. subsidizing upland farming. Those who farm in what the EEC defines as Less Favoured Areas (LFAs) have been given specia
30. it, not only just as well but much better. Weeds have been defined as 'plants in the wrong place.' Wrong, that is, from
31. s of death and dying by statute. At present, 27 states have defined death as the absence of brain function, even though

33. ng and do treatment. In the past the baptism of a child was referred to as 'having the child done'. In similar vein it m
34. went into the house, into the room with the books which was referred to as 'the Study'. Edith, all lowered eyelids and k
35. referred to as the tides, and that is why the phenomenon is referred to as the tidal effect. The tidal effects of bodies
36. eau middle class San Fernando Valley. The place is commonly referred to as the Valley, as in 'Tell me you don't live in
37. not an altogether uncommon name. The film crew, inevitably, referred to him as Comin' and Goin', but Goin was probably w
38. 299.. It was probably among the 'old walls and wild woods' referred to in the tenth century when St Athewold rebuilt th
39. hters.' We all know women of thirty and forty who are still referred to in their family as 'the baby,' or 'the kid.' It
40. nceived notion that this 'do-it-yourself wedding' (as Phil referred to it) was going to be (as Stratton kept predicting

emphasize

1. g tendencies in the ER's model of government. - One formula emphasizes a minimum of government, of interference', and s
2. ve equal rights. And the same applies to school. It must be emphasized again and again that freedom does not involve spo
3. his canons 'only of gain', a point that d'Arcis repeatedly emphasizes. All that was needed was an artist prepared to at
4. tions and pathways that could be made by a normal brain. He emphasized, as a scientist, that his estimate was conservati
5. . Friends did cookery columns from their own recipes, often emphasizing cheapness. We had cosmetic columns about alterna
6. s for a written policy statement on forestry, preferring to emphasize 'cooperation' with professional forestry interests
7. f admirers, and publisher of his writings. Yet one must not emphasize David Jones's isolation too much. One comparison i
8. wants to share his excitements and feels a powerful need to emphasize every point that he considers important. The cynic
9. real help begins by strengthening confidence rather than by emphasizing failure. When I teach a child to read and to wri
10. she loved, or thought she loved. Readers of Jane Austen, he emphasized, gesturing freely with his cigar, should not be m
11. t, I repeat, will not tolerate. In fact . . .' the Minister emphasized his point with pointed forefinger . . . 'he made
12. hance. He must win over the listener and to do this he must emphasize his words over and over again. Bearing this in min
13. ild who is still immature and impressionable. Other mothers emphasize how delicate a girl becomes at such times and how
14. that no one could have dreamed of even a decade ago. I keep emphasizing how dramatically things have changed; this is ne
15. on can do) Why the union? Throughout the book so far, we've emphasized how important it is that working people join unio
16. Hinduism as a unifying cultural force has been increasingly emphasized in sociological studies of pre-European India. Th
17. rs. Wolfert is also an author, a poet. 'A modern poet,' she emphasized. Mr. Lyons paced the lobby, impatient for the bus
18. inflationary pressures. Fed chairman Paul Volcker last week emphasized, once again, that his ultimate goal is to reduce
19. vulgarized, as so many psychiatric terms are, it should be emphasized once more that it is a very precise idea: games s
20. riticizing her or trying to change her mind, he had already emphasized that he was entirely in sympathy with her, and wa
21. n and in subsequent statements, Mr Thompson was at pains to emphasize that he was threatening nobody. Nonetheless, he wa
22. evelopments receive rather more muted enthusiasm the author emphasizes that London is a vital and developing organism, n
23. enormous rewards on investment: super-profits. Others have emphasized that modern imperialism differs sharply from pre-
24. heatre and the ballet company met on Friday, but both sides emphasized that plans are at an early stage. Redevelopment i
25. the others'. Writers on nationalism from Renan onwards have emphasized that: 'races, languages, political traditions and
26. ork by Rosenzweig, as outlined in the chapter on the brain, emphasized that stimulation increased the number of patterns
27. ance of the biased, the misleading and the status quo. Hall emphasizes that the media change the world. They do not pass
28. But he got enough off his chest in this brief encounter to emphasize that there were definitely two schools of thought
29. ged from cramping and bleeding to acute abdominal pain. She emphasized that these symptoms were merely indications that
30. rain pattern' laid down biologically and electrically. They emphasize that this strength is increased by repeating the m
31. foreign affairs. I remembered the conversation with Gus and emphasized that while I am interested in a CIA career I know
32. d so on. Counter Chairman At the beginning of these notes I emphasized the danger, for the lectureman, from his Chairman
33. report said he was not a good security risk,' said Dawlish emphasizing the difference. `My report,' he repeated. `Yes,'
34. ull time route'. In a later speech at Lancaster Mr Crosland emphasized the 'historic and invaluable FE tradition of prov
35. interested in nature. Cole's report, Wildlife in the City, emphasized the importance of creating new wildlife sites in
36. d obligation is very important among the !Kung. Richard Lee emphasizes the point strongly: 'Sharing deeply pervades the
37. it, berries and nuts from low bushes, for instance.' David emphasizes the point that the end product of an evolutionary
38. e significance of a legitimate Opposition, too. But he also emphasizes what liberal Western critics often forget, that t
39. didn't say: 'like men and women in real life.' 'Fowls', he emphasized, 'without their feathers,' and laughed to make it
40. ed costs of pounds 52,000,000 a year; even this, the report emphasized, would require tough restrictive measures at Lond

explain

1. r his kind words on my behalf at the time of my demotion. I explained about Gandar's offer and said it was too good to t
2. eves. As he'd feared, his father became indignant when he'd explained about the rations being deliberately less than the
3. ualize this.' 'Don't put on with me. Don't be superior.' He explained again. 'I'm at the head of the bed, standing. You
4. ot smoking the cigar. It was a problem from my childhood, I explained, and told him about a day back in Virginia when I
5. old lady, Francois immediately set about mollifying her. He explained at length how impossible it had been for him to do
6. araucaria. 'It's a comparatively large house,' he began to explain before remembering: 'Oh, not compared with Sunningda
7. ct between them. 'lt's not that l don't love you any more,' explained Belinda tearfully. 'I do, and I would marry you to
8. nst it. 'I am making a perspective of my house,' the Doctor explained. 'For the house agents.' He was always making gran
9. g, and trains and farewells and all that sort of thing. She explained gently that they had moved out of their bedroom ne
10. oes for several weeks, sought the aid of a psychiatrist. He explained his problem and was told that it was nonsense to a
11. e in anything so basically repellent. He tried to get me to explain how my interest in figures had developed, and took m
12. about Tuesday?' 'Fine. Four o'clock be right for time?' He explained how to get to the hotel where they were to meet, a
13. glanced at them admiringly, and when Jack saw his glance he explained. 'I tried to get over that hill to see if there wa
14. A or ministry vets. Typical battery cages, Clare and Violet explained, measure 18 by 20 1/2 inches ('remember an adult h
15. be almost transparent. 'I've a special old carving-knife,' explained Miss Clare earnestly, 'and I always sharpen it on
16. at she called them,' said Poirot. 'Elephants can remember,' explained Mrs Oliver. 'That was the idea I started on. And p
17. ntricity. Skidding down the hall, the American laughed, and explained: 'My godmother kept cats. The whole of her house i
18. old lady from talking. If she had allowed them to chat, she explained, others would follow suit instead of getting on wi
19. e to court.' He couldn't afford a threeday trip to town, he explained patiently. There would be the cost of searching fo
20. already. That often happened with international flights, he explained; relatives came to see passengers off, and drove t
21. woman in the survey, who came near to a nervous breakdown, explained, 'Staying at home means I'm living with my own fai
22. tomorrow.' 'There are some things she wants from the flat,' explained Stuart. 'Get to California as soon as possible, St
23. s he done?' The young officer was embarrassed. Patiently he explained that he was simply carrrying out instructions. 'Wh
24. een, and I didn't hear him. He repeated the question, and I explained that I was a little deaf from the explosions. He w
25. ere hurried into a private ward off the main ward where she explained that there was a 'mistake' and they now 'wanted to
26. he other end of the phone. The clerk turned to Kowalski and explained that there was no such person. Purely by chance, b
27. 0 sales. John Preston, general manager of Decca Records UK, explained the decision: 'It is obvious that there is an asso
28. eeping down from the house. By building these, Mr Warburton explained, the meditation rooms would be created inside the
29. spent an hour talking with a new student called Kathleen, I explained to her that the tutor I had for her would be new t
30. madness. I suggested very strongly that he see a doctor and explained to him that I was preparing to move, since it was
31. on with the emphasis on physical safety. One social worker explained to me: 'I whisk in, count heads, check the firegua
32. ugh citizen phoning, or STD as we phone people call it,' he explained to me in his office, a phone box in Leicester Squa
33. s healthy and attractive as I can at all times,' Boylan had explained to Rudolph. 'Even if I don't see anybody for weeks
34. en there's the patina,' Mr Boggis continued. 'The what?' He explained to them the meaning of this word as applied to fur
35. bose kindly repeated it. 'It's an Indian name, I guess,' he explained. 'Well, if you haven't been there I'd say you cert
36. few friends just walked in. Hold on.' I grabbed Patterson, explained who was on the line, what we were talking about, a
37. the time he first talked marriage, up in the Mojave. When I explained why not, he went young again. Absurd. He got all o
38. on at a distance could take place', or indeed 'You have not explained why rays of light behave the way they do', he alwa
39. ning. She refused to stay overnight, although she had never explained why. The phone rang and Rudolph picked it up, but
40. d cause for trade retaliation. 'The control of imports,' he explains, 'would not be used to make our balance of payments

give, deliver, issue, make, offer

1   so that the Bomvanas could also watch the eclipse, and Dad gave a final warning to them not to look directly at what th
2   , and I asked him about the girls playing football etc. He gave a surprising answer, 'Have you been listening to the ra
3   e summoned one of the servants with a clap of the hands and gave an order for special food to be brought to Hamo. 'And I
4   clean. He had spent his pocket money on ice cream, and she gave him a lecture about how bad ice cream was for his stoma
5   gloves with holes along the fingers to reveal his rings, he gave his fiance instructions on how to handle the expected c
6   ta likes me!,' and after careful consideration, her parents gave permission for them to marry. Omoro and Binta also agre
7   ell known American Indian, Chief Seattle, doubted this, and gave the following advice to the 'white man' in his speech o
8   note of urgency in it. The light was growing as he promptly gave the word to move, on the internal radio channel, with t
9
10 ave that clock alone,' Lionel said, feeling it incumbent to deliver a parting shot at the door. 'You know what you're li
11   elected second in the constituency section - Harold Wilson delivered a speech which was a masterpiece of ambiguity, ost
12   about the history of the place. After twelve months here I deliver a well-rehearsed answer in my classroom Hebrew. The
13 earance in 1778 when he came, mortally ill, to the Lords to deliver an impassioned appeal against the dismemberment of t
14 s, you have gone right up, you snooty little bitch; she had delivered her comments with her back to him, busy with a fil
15 en, as they are affectionately called, meet twice a year to deliver judgment on their validity, as a body, and to descri
16 d, of the bomb's power. The atomic scientists in New Mexico delivered their opinion: 'We can propose no technical demons
17
18 ion and finding herself quite incapable of dealing with it, issued a flustered invitation to Ash to join their party tha
19 session of expert photographers who checked every stage and issued a notarized statement that his work was free from any
20 U.S. Attorney General and the President's campaign manager, issued a statement: 'The person involved is the proprietor o
21 g of Three', was issued on 7June. Yet although they had now issued a threat to leave the Labour Party, none of the three
22 e who worked with the Americans shook his head. 'Truman has issued absolute orders that the United States is not to pres
23 Admiral Garrland, who refused to take the responsibility of issuing an order to board the Exodus. Trevor-Browne knew tha
24 a decade ago the United Nations Secretary-General, U Thant, issued the following warning: 'The members of the United Nat
25
26   wall, which is all most heartening. Mrs Pringle, to whom I made a blithe comment about the fine weather, did her best t
27   fight for my job. Virtually every person with whom I spoke made a firm promise to observe the general strike and to att
28 e situation and what treatment may be needed. Twins: I once made an appeal to mothers of twins to tell me what solutions
29 noise'. Darling, whatever's the matter?' Still staring, she made no answer. I went across to her. 'Karin! What is it?' '
30 ver the period of one year. We presume, since no mention is made of any student comment, that the student's assessment o
31 e university. He knew about the many threats which had been made on my life and was concerned for my safety. George was
32 down the Government. In a powerful and emotional appeal, he made the call for a fresh start with a plain recognition tha
33   able to tell whether any man was bewitched or not. He also made the rather curious statement that there were three kind
34
35 ed in the subversion of his own principles. The excuse he'd offered himself at the time - that the hours of chit-chat we
36 I was just doing what I was told' was the usual explanation offered in interviews held after the experiment. To rebut th
37 readers to books and keeps them reading. The advice usually offered is 'match the book to the reader' and those who have
38 he cortex.) Despite the fact of his observation, Herophilus offered no reason for his conclusion. It was not until the 1
39 o know why I had referred to Sister Eugenius in this way, I offered the imaginative explanation that what I had said was
40   than knocks him over. 'Drive and dive' is the usual advice offered to those planning a rear tackle. The drive is very i

go, have it, run

1. eve hard enough. 'You can't get there from here' the cliche went. But you could. I was getting there. In the dressing ro
2. ted that he should come in on a good deal. The conversation went like this: 'Well, just take my word, it's a good deal.
3. at this, there are only two Andropov jokes. Joke number one goes like this. Lackey to Andropov: 'Comrade Andropov, how d
4. traight through it. An extract from my diary of that period goes like this: 'Conditions here are dreadful. Nowhere to ea
5. come into conflict. In this process, people (as the phrase goes) can wear different hats: the civil servant who defends
6. ect of machine thought is first broached, a common reaction goes something like this: 'What a horrible idea! How could a
7. ylan,' she said flatly. 'Is he still alive?' 'So the rumour goes,' Rudolph said. 'I haven't seen him for a long time, ei
8. ad who have no desire to weaken them. But as the old saying goes, 'The road to hell is paved with good intentions', and
9. most of the emotions that today pass for love. As the song goes: At seventeen I fell in love quite madly With eyes of a
10. ies irrelevant to the days of the E E C. If only, the story goes, people in Northern Ireland would take up more of the g
11. ' They were the only ones left in his bag - or so the story goes! Sometimes inadvertently you drive from in front of th
12. t six weeks more to run. There was a joke going around that went like this: 'What's the difference between the Marine Co
13. Jenny went around for a week sort of singing a jingle that went 'Jonas, Marsh and Barrett.' I told her not so fast and
14. days, he had to memorize a definition of a preposition that went something like this: 'A preposition is a word, generall
15. itting in the sun. There's an old San Francisco saying that goes: 'It's better to rest in Washington Square than in the
16. get to the senior, they will all work harder (so the theory goes) to prove how efficient and responsible they can be in
17. I'm staring at while I'm feeling good. Only by doing this, goes the theory, can the male be seduced into rushing off an
18. s point, he may decide to have a little talk with you which goes something like this: 'Now, Veronica, I know you've made
19.
20. ess. Sometimes the new man had 'emerged', as the expression had it, as though he was a kind of Botticelli Venus or Excal
21. nd Belvoir. Lascelles was much in love with her, but gossip had it that she would marry Granby. I do not believe that su
22. rs, the police, law schools. Nada. The standing office joke had it that Bernstein heard the whole Watergate story and mu
23. tive too much for you, then stay out of the kitchen. Legend has it that when a new beer is tried out in Munich it is pos
24. e otherwise; to 'think for ourselves' as the common phrase has it, and to 'stand on our own feet' without the support o
25. ew that Woodward couldn't write very well. One office rumor had it that English was not Woodward's native language. But
26. had left off, at least, his heavy gold necklace that, rumor had it, was solid gold, a gift from an admirer in Italy; he
27. time I had taken my young to swim at my neighbour's. Rumour had it that he didn't like children, but I ignored the canar
28. ve ever heard of this,' he said, 'but one school of thought has it that there are people with a kind of extra-sensory pe
29. thirteenth century — to repel the Mongols. Or so tradition has it; certainly the Mongols at that time repeatedly tried
30.
31. nd. 'As they had breakfast in the same room' the allegation runs, 'he could have done it in the hotel.' That complaint w
32. st society are victims of sexual oppression' - the argument runs, in its most extreme form - 'which is exploited by the
33. enly displayed in the press—'Brolly attack on mother-to-be' ran the Evening News headline. The Daily Telegraph was, as u
34. be paid for in humiliation. 'No sons begets many children,' runs another Chinese proverb: the family that has no luck al
35. t was an unfamiliar educated hand. He quickly opened it. It ran as follows. Dear Tim, Please forgive me for writing to y
36. e effects of such ravages. 'Enjoy your age - don't look it' runs one advertisement. My aged friends are fortunate if the
37. a slide of Dennis and Elsie quarrelling. The teacher's note runs as follows: 'The classic opposition across the frame of
38. ly widely believed - and equally unscientific - saying that runs: 'Fifty million Frenchmen can't be wrong'. And most of
39. earing that she is a Lloyd's broker. 'The questions usually run, 'Which branch and do you get a special cheque book?', a
40. experiment of reading verses from it to children. One verse runs: Tommy saw his house on fire, His mother in the flames

insist

1 zi plot . ' 'Paul Bock gained access to the bank computer,' insisted Boyd Stuart. 'The other one has worked in electroni
2 ell me a story,' he said. 'You tell me one,' said I. No, he insisted, he could not tell me a story; I must tell him one.
3 manager of the Nixon campaign, explaining that his wife had insisted he quit. Woodward asked several members of the Post
4 et expression. I asked him if she exerted pressure, but he insisted he was there of his own choice. I am touched by the
5 ere must have been some woman you never told me about,' she insisted. He would have to get away from Nance: the smell of
6 t least, that's what the captain said.' 'For five hours,' I insisted, 'I have been trying to make a phone call, and ever
7 ife. 'I'm sure,' said Murdo. 'I'm telling the truth,' Janet insisted. 'I'm not denying it,' said Murdo as he watched the
8 my watch, my comb, and even my wedding ring, which they had insisted I should take off. My clothes had been returned to
9 (whose presence always seemed to offend him personally). He insisted I was not to attend or participate in anything that
10 oncert on Wednesday night. One is for myself, the other, she insists, is for you. She says she met you on a bus. I told h
11 station had suddenly disappeared. Yet at the same time, she insisted, many of her friends had taken forthright positions
12 It depends what you're used to, though. 'Shetland's great,' insisted Margaret, an oil wife. She lives in one of the oil
13 children's faces. 'You have to find some compromise,' Sammy insisted. 'Maybe sell the house and buy a trailer. After for
14 ere paragraph from her stewardess manual, which the company insisted must be read on every flight. 'On behalf of Captain
15 ack. Inside two years I knew there would be a compromise. I insisted on a contract that gave me some sort of job for lif
16 ust have references for everyone they supply. Many agencies insist on an interview before a mother's help joins a family
17 e said push. When Barbara went into Leeds Infirmary, Howard insisted on being present. Indeed when the day came at last,
18 should cancel the whole thing. And the trouble was that he insisted on coming to the airport to see her off. 'Dear God,
19 g climbed with Jim, felt little confidence in him either. I insisted on doing a training climb first, and the next morni
20 tory you have already read to him and he has enjoyed. Don't insist on every word being exact. Encourage him to tell the
21 himself collect the cash-some six thousand dollars which he insisted on having sewn into the lining of his jacket; for s
22 ect her this week at all,' said the harassed husband, 'I am insisting on her staying in bed for at least three days. She
23 mpany tax was stiffened, wage-increases of 20 per cent were insisted on, plus an increased investment locally of 60 per
24 of the Don. This edict was completely disregarded. The Don insisted on the council of war being held in his room at the
25 een simulated. There was also family pressure. Alice Keppel insisted on the marriage taking place, and Violet adored her
26 t protested it was impractical and not her style at all. He insisted she make an appointment at the beauty salon in thei
27 hat she was deliberately not getting a garbage disposal. He insisted she tell him why. A bit of reflection caused her to
28 er, but couldn't get past his answering device. The sheriff insisted stonily that this had nothing to do with anyone but
29 motivation that makes a father who had no musical education insist that his son learn to play the piano. And it makes a
30 who had now found another way to make my life a misery. She insisted that I should thoroughly clean the cooker every day
31 again. After Johnny dropped Hagen off at the airport (Hagen insisted that Johnny not hang around for his plane with him)
32 hree). He had mentioned it to his daughter Jennifer but she insisted that she didn't mind. The marriage is all over and
33 with an apple in his mouth. Apparently the gateman, having insisted that the box be opened, prodded the animal dubiousl
34 s. Many more people resent the idea of lateral thinking and insist that vertical thinking is quite sufficient. In fact,
35 to let them wear them through the snow to school, she still insisted that when they arrived they had to change into skir
36 to bring home as a child? The story was a fabrication, she insisted. Then, what about the Black boyfriend? Her daughter
37 But I can only record that senior members of the hierarchy insisted to me they were not trying to run the country, and
38 r and had walked slowly with her along the ground floor and insisted upon buying her a suede handbag for fifteen dollars
39 the uncles offered in exchange for their nephews' favours, insisted upon the whole company sitting down to a game of Mo
40 was aware she'd done so. 'Yes, but there's a difference,' I insisted. 'You wanted a college in the East, and I didn't. I

is, are, was, were, been

1   n' used to say, 'Taxi No thanks. The Ministry is sending or is alleged to be sending a car for me.' When everybody had
2   comfortable room temperature is 18-20 degrees C. The house is assumed not to require heat until the average external t
3   of a burglary of which the objective was her jewellery. He is believed to have fled to Paris and to be hiding here. Al
4   urch you will find, behind the screen at the west end, what is claimed to be the oldest arch in the City of London, of
5   be wise to have a look at technology itself. If technology is felt to be becoming more and more inhuman, we might do w
6   nest monkeys in India, often living around temples where it is held to be sacred. Farther east still, a species has bec
7   s never been caught to this day, Georges Watin got away and is presumed to be living in Spain along with most of the ot
8   ion by the Senate would be the making of him. 'For,' Irving is reported to have said, 'there is such a thing in politic
9   ardens recall the long gone Rose Theatre (where Shakespeare is said to have acted) and the Hope Theatre on the old bear
10 ty. That is why today, for example, more than sixty nations are alleged to use torture systematically as a political in
11 ing a design solution. Creative design and practical skills are believed to be of great importance and are taught by me
12 ever, precautions taken in early 1975 to prevent root death are claimed to have been successful so far. Little is known
13 ted into our environment by a nuclear explosion, only a few are considered to be really harmful so far as internal cont
14 sefully diversify the mixture - may be dropped because they are felt to be too expensive. Since money is a very importa
15 egal experts in this form of recovery. Unfortunately, there are known to be a handful of people - they amount to certai
16 elsewhere, some of which have been promising, while others are known to have failed. All these experiments should be g
17 es than in Japan. Even Japan's big life insurance companies are reckoned to have taken more interest in American bonds.
18 leasant one s, and dreams involving fear, anger and sadness are reported to occur twice as often as dreams in which the
19 al or intellectual growth. Partners in successful marriages are said to 'grow together.' This 'parallel development' th
20 r centuries it was the centre of Celtic Christianity. There are said to have been three hundred and sixty large stone c
21 ess, please; I'll send you pictures of three of the men who are supposed to be doing the killings. They're old pictures
22 Who could even name them? And if these venerable, old ideas are thought not to be worth bothering about, what new ideas
23 salad vegetables contain substances such as vitamin C which are thought to help prevent stomach cancer, possibly by sto
24 earlier, about the time of Geoffrey I, when the same cloth was claimed quite openly to be the true Shroud by the canon
25 they might work together with their common aim. Such a body was felt to be valuable for the exchange of ideas it would
26 proportion of overall suicides. Among white males the rate was found to be six times greater among old people than in
27 ge had been introduced to an ancient and sleepy lion, who was guaranteed to obey anybody who cracked a whip at him, a
28 bal display went on among these clever modern children. Tim was judged by them all to be more monstrous than any; and K
29 -5 billion a year in precious foreign exchange. This figure was predicted to rise six-fold by 1980. And the technology
30 ay.   All this while no more had been seen of Snowball. He was rumoured to be hiding on one of the neighbouring farms,
31 . An attractive older student, a woman in her mid-thirties, was said to have abandoned her doctoral dissertation and to
32 of the power of men and how to take it from them. Politics was taken to mean socialism, and theory the extension of Ma
33 inuing cycle of a family or a people or the world. The dead were believed to come back to their old homes at Halloween,
34 e only six such units in the country. Ten years later there were estimated to be 239 such units. In 1979 the DES made a
35 chael how his business had gone. Even such polite questions were understood to be awkward, not that he wouldn't give he
36 ow what nutrition is all about. Vitamin E, for example, has been claimed to protect people against all sorts of complai
37 ch food then produces the poison called aflatoxin which has been found to cause cancer in animal experiments (see Chapt
38 the huge sea-gong species that lives in Southeast Asia have been reported to be over 6 metres long. Fossil crocodiles a
39 , it was considered to be an accident, and the children had been said to be playing together, pushing each other, etcet
40 e looked very much worse than it was. Perhaps it had always been thought to be unclimbable. Whatever the hell they thou

it

1. eeper accommodations and food in a dining car. Furthermore, it is understood and agreed that the Ministry pay all expen
2. mber of persons allowed into each office and classroom, and it was alleged that the windows on the West side were seale
3. n dioxide has been rising steadily for the last century and it is feared that this will upset the delicate balance. A c
4. arlier wars, when shaving must have been just as difficult. It has also been suggested that American men were imitating
5. clear war is unlikely to be an essentially terminal event.' It has just been revealed that the Pentagon is already plan
6. with the peculiar problems of this country. Few cricketers, it has to be said, positively look forward to visiting Paki
7. d not been explained to the Group. Because of this feeling, it was decided to invite Vic Feather to speak to the Group
8. ing visual attribute is the sky. You can see the whole sky, it is said. To be honest, I am not at all sure I want to se
9. bury colleagues' work. In contrast, these English pictures, it must be admitted, are a little sad, a little drab; paint
10. he legalization of casinos, which was also part of the Act. It was stipulated in the legislation that all players shoul
11. normal way. Barbara addressed the meeting on the Bill, and it was agreed to call a further meeting on the 10th. On thi
12. her man dead for three weeks before anyone discovered him. It was reported that four different men had died this lonel
13. . Living away from home creates many of these problems, and it is hoped that those who have difficulty in coping will s
14. was completed in record time and six weeks after census day it was announced that the population of the USA stood at 62
15. f technique. At the end of their courses the students will (it is asserted) not only understand the extent and signific
16. le will the runner be encouraged to restrengthen this area. It cannot be stressed too highly that if muscles are streng
17. e already had an airport, which did only a little business; it was proposed to extend it vastly and make it suitable fo
18. er the farming and fishery industries. Good administration, it can be argued, cannot flow from a government Ministry ch
19. the expectations that are being aroused all over the world, it appears to be assumed that within a few decades most peo
20. nd follows last month's visit by President Sadat of Egypt. It had earlier been expected that the White House meetings
21. suit should be washed to remove chemicals used in spraying. It is usually recommended to wait until the age of 2 to add
22. gage in this tactic is, therefore, of limited significance. It should be mentioned here that it would probably not be n
23. dge Woolsey added a waggish touch. 'Furthermore,' he said, 'it must always be remembered that Joyce's locale is Celtic
24. asic units which facilitate description of complex figures. It has been noted how these larger units, because of their
25. raeli facilities for the American rapid deployment force, it was disclosed yesterday. The moves suggest that the R
26. ws. Our democracy makes laws - good ones, too. For example, it is forbidden to bathe in the sea without the supervision
27. wspaper readers to form their own opinions of their worth'. It has never been denied that Price was the author of the N
28. e stayed on 'our' side of the line (the east side) they let it be known we would be left in peace. If we ever crossed o
29. irst time he did it I thought he was having a heart attack. It became known at the bar that I was from 'South Afrika',
30. diseases might also be caused by infections. In experiments it has been shown many times that animals, including mice,
31. d not penetrate my gloom. By the time I was ready to leave, it was decided that none of the old men wanted to come. Tha
32. of the telephone line by cutting them off in mid-sentence. It was rumoured that he collected the phone numbers of like
33. y through incorporation of new social values. Consequently, it has been claimed, the right mode of analysis is a kind o
34. ng around their table waiting to start their deliberations, it was discovered that there were no translators. Now, noth
35. th of them. They were comrades with a special relationship. It had long been established that they suited each other, a
36. s rumoured to have a second, half-African family). And then it began to be said that Noimon would regret his decision.
37. cording to their various skills and abilities. In this way, it is felt, the children have an education which is much mo
38. ich come within the diet. Sugar is allowed in the diet, but it has been pointed out that sugar is not essential to a ba
39. start the Unit had to be closed down due to lack of funds. It is, however, hoped to revive it again in the future. A l
40. sh vegetables and wheat-grains and raw foods such as salad. It has been estimated that the average family throws away p

laugh, gasp, groan, moan, sigh, sob

1. pointedly. 'Because I'm inquisitive by nature,' the printer laughed - and admitted, 'may I ask your name and line of bu
2. he mule story'?' Burr looked blank. ' 'Mule story'? Oh,' he laughed. 'I tell it only to children. You are much too big
3. ight. Stay a week or two' 'I can't do that, I'm afraid,' he laughed. 'I'm due in Oxford next week. I go up on Tuesday.'
4. rned an indelible black. 'You can't scrub it off,' Don Card laughed. 'It only wears out when the skin-layer wears off.'
5. dryly, 'I noticed it when you came into the room.' 'Lord,' laughed Jack, 'I'm sorry if I gave you that impression.' 'I
6. d simply walked through the front gate unchallenged, and he laughed: 'You may not see them, but they're there.' He show
7.
8. r sure. I may be all wrong.' 'Tell me what you do know,' he gasped 'All right, this is what I think. The bullet entered
9. precise scientific terms.) She reeled - sitting down - and gasped, 'All that raw egg white will kill him.' 'What's wit
10. o not let go, whatever you do !.' 'I am holding on, ma'am,' gasped Fanny between chattering teeth —chattering from the
11. When they informed my landlady, she was appalled. 'Oh,' she gasped, 'he must be so cold. Couldn't one of you lend him a
12. hat's the matter with you?' Claud asked. 'It's nothing,' he gasped. 'I'll be all right in a minute. Please - a glass of
13. her neck look brittle. 'That was my painting,' she said, or gasped. 'You never looked at it.' He could have flattened h
14.
15. to the bungalow at that. Talk sense.' 'I believe I am mad,' groaned George, striking his forehead in a manner that woul
16. oke. 'Say, think of a number !' 'Eleven-hundred and two,' I groaned, in a trance. 'Double it,' he hissed in my ear. Dou
17. sounded like an old crow's. Piero appeared. 'I'm sick,' he groaned. 'I've got fever. I think I'm dying. Get me some ho
18. dlines. POLICE PROBE PIES FOR MISSING WlFE. 'Oh my God,' he groaned. 'This is going to do our public image no end of go
19. rying to sell us a life insurance policy.' 'Oh no,' Laverne groaned. 'You didn't buy one?' Eddie asked. 'I consider the
20. pillow, took in Judy wearing a sari and her hair in a bun, groaned 'You look awful,' and then wearily sank back again.
21.
22. ry land.' 'I'll never see the land again. God help us all,' moaned Amy O'Shea and gave a dreadful gasp and covered her
23. rthought, added: 'We'll look after him.' 'Where is he?' she moaned. 'He's my husband, my husband. I want to see him.' '
24. gain in somebody's back yard. 'You've lost me ball!' Angela moaned, her ripe-banana skin sweating worse than ever. 'We
25. fered a fresh outbreak of woe. 'What am I going to do?' she moaned. 'In Melbourne!' 'We'll write to each other' - he tr
26. down on to her bed. She held her head between her hands and moaned to herself, 'This is just too awful.' 'Of course it'
27.
28. things. 'I asked them never to give me squash,' Mr. Solomon sighed, 'and here it is again.' Mrs. Babcock - whom Ginny h
29. hatever cost. 'Oh I never never could do such a thing,' she sighed. 'But thank you for making the offer. It was very ki
30. to me,' said Sutherland. Trevor-Browne poured some tea and sighed, half embarrassed, 'See here, Bruce. If it were up t
31. mouth moved, but didn't succeed in articulating. 'Oh!' she sighed. 'I'd like to fall in love - with somebody appropria
32. ind until we have studied this document.' 'Poor Mr Miller,' sighed the butcher's wife, 'he came into our shop last week
33. s wife, closing the window firmly. 'She's right, you know,' sighed the vicar sadly to the cat which came up to rub his
34.
35. u want to hear about my idea?' 'Oh, Albert, I'm tired,' she sobbed. 'I'm so tired I don't know what I'm doing any more.
36. to tears - which is rare with her. 'I hate everything!' she sobbed. 'Me, too?' But Helen only blew her nose; splashed c
37. remembrance hit her and her eyes bulged and she turned and sobbed, 'My baby . . . my baby . . .' She sat up slowly. Jo
38. had half killed yourself.' 'It hurts, it hurts dreadfully!' sobbed Patty, hoisted to her feet by the unsympathetic Mart
39. becoming acute. I tried to talk to George, but he wept and sobbed that he wanted to go home. 'This is just a prison,'
40. h's beard. Thirteen pounds. 'Twelve and that's final.' Akim sobbed that he was being cheated but he was a poor Arab so

order

1. not because she would be late since, these days, she always ordered a cab for a good half-hour earlier than ought to be
2. nel. Everything was perfectly normal. 'Open outer door,' he ordered. Again Hal repeated his instructions; at any stage,
3. n the earlier erroneous FBI reports. Although the judge had ordered all televisions removed from the jurors' motel room
4. ondonderry's grim Bogside district, housewife Bridgin Cooke ordered an extra delivery of coal, saying, 'If we need milk
5. Kinley and Sherman were cajoled into receiving her. Sherman ordered an investigation into her husband's death. All news
6. On one of these rivers was a sort of Noah's ark that I had ordered built the previous year. My house-boat was about si
7. er one in the morning, took off his immaculate dark jacket, ordered coffee from the night staff, and rang for his assis
8. been impossible. They were both such eccentrics. They kept ordering each other out of the theatre with Shaw in the mid
9. nly the engine stopped. The sergeant in charge of the class ordered everybody to take cover under the desks. 'My mind w
10. r bodies to move their thin blood. As dawn broke the guards ordered everyone to their feet. Some didn't get to their fe
11. debated with himself for a while, then called a florist and ordered flowers sent to Georgetown Hospital. He was concern
12. u Yesha,' he said, He clapped his ringed hands together and ordered fruit and coffee to be brought to the strangers, As
13. Finally, satisfied that he was far away from the reefs, he ordered, 'Hard right rudder! Full speed ahead!' and the Cor
14. the only response I could muster to her catastrophe. But I ordered her some flowers, roses, red ones, and that appease
15. he landlord had found out that she had deceived him and had ordered her to vacate her apartment. She had promised this
16. asked he obvious question. But Sloan would not say who had ordered him to make the secret payments. He wanted more tim
17. up a tiny vacant table at the open window of Pierre's cafe, ordered himself an ice-cream and Irish coffee, and sat back
18. ' she said 'Bring her a sandwich and some milk,' Sutherland ordered his servant.'Now see here, young lady, what is all
19. uffered them at regular intervals. 'Come here,' Doctor Farr ordered. I rose from the sofa where I habitually spent bili
20. lear weapons materials. Like teaching a child to walk then ordering it not to....Sam took a short cut...In 1957 he can
21. ational, an engine overheated. As a precaution, the captain ordered it shut down. None of the aircraft's pas- sengers w
22. er son's advancement. 'At whatever cost, he must be found,' ordered Janoo-Rani. 'He and his mother both, for he will ha
23. sely private man, shutting himself away in his hotel room, ordering meals to be sent up and not emerging until it is t
24. umalism or not, Lieutenant Donovan felt it was sabotage and ordered no information to be given out beyond routine relea
25. gaze at the little patch of dark wood. 'Feel it!' Mr Boggis ordered. 'Put your fingers on it! There, how does it feel,
26. ron, sometime dictator of Argentina by popular acclamation, ordered that it should be taught in all schools. I admit to
27. he last moment to accompany him to New York. The Chief also ordered that the picture must be published the next day in
28. ; it was unusual in a man. Parker said, 'General Zhadov has ordered that the Stein documents are top priority. Nothing
29. ght,' the judge said now, almost in a state of panic, 'I am ordering that the trial be moved to San Francisco.' With th
30. mothers intended leaving them overnight, the prime minister ordered that they be taken to women's prisons. That would s
31. the cat, who had suddenly disappeared just before Napoleon ordered the animals to assemble. For some time nobody spoke
32. ut after a few minutes - bored or fearful - the parents had ordered the children back up the beach: Brody heard footste
33. indignation that 'here they have created a sanatorium' and ordered the director 'to tighten things up': the registered
34. our funds before my son takes me home. Go away, Basil,' she ordered the poor man, who had stepped forward to take her a
35. day of great violence. Yesterday the Minister of Government ordered the release of the five students but they refused t
36. he phoned him. He asked to speak to Phil and then furiously ordered them both to leave his mother's apartment at once.
37. layed behind the counter wore dark glasses. 'Bring him in,' ordered Thomas, 'and get back here yourself.' Then he picke
38. o see her. Their patience became exhausted and she was next ordered to contact me and ask me to see her at the apartmen
39. tion to his officers. Luckily for his own reputation he was ordered to Egypt early in August to take command of the bel
40. whom the local police were searching. At first Jed was only ordered to steal small sums of money from his parents. Kasp

order, promise, proposal, request, suggestion

1. was no answer to that, and Ash never knew who had given the order that he was not to be allowed to leave : the Rajah, or
2. -documented motions were filed, the judge finally issued an order that legal investigators of our designation be admitte
3. m. On January 3, 1942, President Quezon issued an executive order that $500,000 be transferred from the account of the P
4. bomb craters and along the sides of hedges, waiting for the order to attack. The 6th Airborne's commander, General Gale,
5. ke a night journey deep into the surrounding forest. At the order to march, the long line of boys set out along the path
6. erty is sacred. Much praised was President Jackson's recent order to the postmasters to destroy any abolitionist literat
7.
8. f crucial safety questions in time for the Inquiry, despite promises by Ministers that this would be done. FoE cross-exa
9. I'll come to you!' At this point Gorbanevskaya recalled her promise not to cause suffering to her mother, and yielded. S
10. Paget, father of the twins, returned to England, with vague promises of presently sending for them, he had left Manuela,
11. ince February is approaching, this is to remind you of your promise of three paintings for my mixed show. The others, so
12. ith an allowance in one of his villas outside Imola, with a promise that he would recognise any child that might be born
13. together - even Alec, who had either forgotten his original promise to buy fish and chips, or was just more impressed by
14. win them over. . . .' Stein was about to add that MacIver's promise to get Billy a job in the movie industry was a good
15.
16. that, in the example above, there is another issue - say, a proposal for better street lighting - on which the other vot
17. or the provision for children, the final report contained a proposal that family allowances should not be paid to the fi
18. elf - unsatisfied. Helen was in a bad mood made worse by my proposal that she move out of Thomas Street. 'Where on earth
19. which was heightened by the University's opposition to the proposal that some or all of the colleges should be raised t
20. papers. 'A rather contentious item,' he says, introducing a proposal that the number of student representatives be incre
21. had just told her: that he had refused Mr Feibergerstein's proposal to send them home to work out the last year of his
22. and that of any dependants have been made on your behalf. A proposal to study only part-time, for instance at evening cl
23.
24. al laundries. In March 1972 he approached the Centre with a request for assistance in the making of a good quality paper
25. urgoyne and his army in the north. With the good news was a request from Gates that the bearer be promoted to brigadier-
26. to the courthouse. But there was no verdict at hand, only a request from the jury to have some of the evidence delivered
27. an return the boeuf Stroganoff to the chef with a courteous request that he should try again, and if he is prepared to d
28. iss authorities that you are aboard this aircraft, with the request that this information be relayed to the Ministry of
29. Sedburgh. So it seemed probable that he would view Julie's request to go to Art College with favour, involving as it di
30. sufficiently anxious about her job at NBC to pass on their request to me to explain the mission, its purpose, whether i
31.
32. one of the clubs. He never went to bed before dawn. So the suggestion of a four A.M. meeting was not as outlandish as i
33. gan to feel hungry. I was thinking seriously of Uncle Sam's suggestion of leaving home - going, perhaps, to London, or e
34. he cries from the garden, she and Miss Jackson agreed to my suggestion that coffee in the sitting-room would be pleasant
35. rring, professor of theoretical physics in Vienna, made the suggestion that he should give up his chair in Vienna and go
36. de?' said the Count. He spoke stiffly, formally. Gertrude's suggestion that he was angry was indeed not far from the tru
37. studentship automatically and had accepted his Professor's suggestion that he write an MA thesis on the juvenilia of Ja
38. m mild to extreme. For instance, in 'How to spend money' my suggestion that you try having two purses may help you solve
39. p a limited company for Spare Rib and allocated shares. The suggestion to call the magazine Spare Rib was originally a j
40. o it for the money you see.' He'd been enthusiastic about a suggestion to try the zoo for a possible job and we kept it

persuade, convince, dissuade

1 t with honeyed words. Mrs Pringle had allowed herself to be persuaded against such a dire decision and returned to her
2 ris. In that order.' He spent another hour on the phone and persuaded both men to leave their beds and get back to thei
3 and she could no longer work at her profession. Finally she persuaded her husband to sell the grocery store and they re
4 ce a day or two before and, finding her in low spirits, had persuaded her to join them for the sake of a change of air.
5 oy and British troops governing the land. Sita had tried to persuade herself that the man was mistaken, or lying. For i
6 ith someone else.' I looked at him thinking should I try to persuade him out of it, say, you don't want me brooding all
7 examine that Rolex?' It took another quarter of an hour to persuade him that the Rolex was not contraband; then he beg
8 Seville that year – 1491 – on a sales trip; he had come to persuade Queen Isabella to back his voyages but could not g
9 gone, though they were much higher, of course. Seems Heyter persuaded Smith to carry on, said he'd be all right, he'd a
10 will be lowered by some $95; conversely, consumers must be persuaded that black is a desirable colour to have. The spi
11 is is to some extent a circular problem: households must be persuaded that it is worthwhile to save for home-ownership
12 Cambridge crap,' Alan said. 'Winston Spencer Churchill. He persuaded the British they were still the tops, they still
13 on handcuffing Goin, Heissman and even the wounded Otto. I persuaded them that the Count was not a danger and further
14 hink happened? Wily Smith harangued his fellow students and persuaded them that they must support the strike by boycott
15 d. 'Did you persuade Rex and his mother not to sell?' 'I've persuaded them to hold on for the time being. I think if th
16 in silver or gold. It is not hard to see how the Regent was persuaded. Then in 1717, Law organized the Company of the W
17 the matter up again. In the years after Kathy left, he was persuaded to allow two exhibitions of his more recent works
18 ry supported him, also Amanda. Hilary allowed herself to be persuaded. Took a shower, washed her hair, and changed into
19 ible he will want to discuss the matter with you and try to persuade you to change your mind. However, men are not note
20
21 ith the elections in June, Chiriboga has since been able to convince Basantes of the continuing need for his 'advice'.
22 caught him? by the bus stop. For Clive's sake, Dirk had to convince Clive to come in and talk. We were the only people
23 Room of the City Hotel. 'Oh, it took me hours and hours to convince her that I did have an aunt who lived here and tha
24 o each other on Sundays, after the Saturday visit), and she convinced herself that he had had a car accident on the mot
25 en I spoke to him, he told me that it was Jefferson who had convinced him that he should appeal directly to the people;
26 tions which can locate him, He would come back if you could convince him that Karen needs him.' Ari blew a stream of sm
27 home was the last thing I wanted to do but A.C. and Bernard convinced me it was the only sensible course to take and im
28 d her husband look really down and out. What she said to me convinced me more than anything else that we'd succeeded. I
29 all to employer and begins the second part of the sale - to convince Mr Y that Miss X is just the person he needs. To d
30 everything still happening in its own place. I have almost convinced our friend, Miss Judy Marston, of this. She shoul
31 ho had got it in turn from a college roommate. The book had convinced Serjeant to drop out of college and take (briefly
32 hing that seems to, you know, apply.' 'How are you going to convince Simonius to go along with this?' she asked. 'I am
33 bother you, we should not trouble you. So Rose had tried to convince them it was a serious matter, and had succeeded, a
34 d White Horse refused to sign, but Bent took them aside and convinced them it was the only way to keep their power and
35
36 not all potential readers discover them. Some are actively dissuaded by parents who want them to read the classics - -
37 ss. I had thought this highly hypocritical and had tried to dissuade David from going, but he just looked at me as if I
38 , for a time, for the present. Anne had felt it her duty to dissuade Gertrude from an unworthy marriage. Now she felt i
39 n South Africa and would emigrate to Australia. We tried to dissuade him, but his mind was made up. His departure was a
40 gh, at all events, for some of his fellow cadets to try and dissuade him from going into the Indian Army - especially n

point out

1. near Holland during the war. In one of his reports Mark had pointed out a British tactical blunder that had caused a re
2. ch individual case. He cites examples of confused minds and points out a variety of possible causes which have been tot
3. to trail after him. There was in any case, the small voice pointed out, absolutely no one else. The Bilge Lab was part
4. after all these years, especially if you've got a family,' points out Agnes. 'It takes courage to lift the phone.' And
5. ed at him. 'It's a golden opportunity, really,' Reichmeider pointed out, 'and he'll only come at you another night if y
6. economically only as providing positions. Elsewhere, Comte pointed out another 'obvious' impossibility: we could never
7. ght be more significance to the flowers. 'Most of them,' he points out, 'are known to have herbal properties and are us
8. year, and billed.' Most businessmen who travelled, Demerest pointed out, had at least one of the credit cards he had na
9. ncreased weight and decreased airline revenue. The FAA, Mel pointed out, had made a study of airport insurance and subs
10. f the party go back to Fairacre.' 'But tomorrow is Sunday!' pointed out his wife. 'Upon my word,' said the vicar, turni
11. ed impossible that they could be the work of any artist. He pointed out how difficult and pointless it would have been
12. ry, a fogy, a brick-bat stuck in the wheels of progress. He pointed out how the Doctor's philosophy was an encouragemen
13. over millennia. In traditional Hindu thought, an authority points out, 'individual rights are related to the performan
14. rged, 'and get your exit permit.' 'What we need, surely,' I pointed out, 'is an entry pemit.' 'True,' said the guard, '
15. both sides of every major issue. In many cases, the author pointed out, 'it is nobody's business to put the other side
16. lities and even carrying on interesting conversations. Good points out it might be necessary to teach the computer some
17. ke the Jackal on their files. Without such co-operation, he pointed out, it would be impossible even to start looking.
18. kov anticipates the reader criticizing him for naivete, and points out: 'It should not be forgotten that it was, after
19. ll pay to the limit of her capacity', which the Mail rudely pointed out meant anything or nothing. Northcliffe was dema
20. dley. 'There's not a soul will stand for it!' 'And anyway,' pointed out Mr Roberts, 'who wants to pay for something he
21. arce in arable eastern England. Nature reserves, the report pointed out, occupied only 0.8% of Great Britain, and only
22. two coins. 'That 50 pence piece has been there all day,' I pointed out. 'Oh, well,' he said, 'ten pee then. Can I have
23. t. We came in to a very fierce lecture from the captain who pointed out, rightly, that we should have stayed to turn th
24. also a good mathematician. He agreed with my reasoning, but pointed out that anyone can develop the mathematical facult
25. that these handicaps caused him to be alone in the world. I pointed out that he spent his week-ends with me, his days w
26. ew things clear before we go.' He had already told them, he pointed out, that legal proceedings must be the basis of a
27. ould reduce fat consumption by 7 per cent. The James Report points out that milk fat is mostly saturated fat (one of th
28. he title includes a question mark. Dealing with strikes, he points out that most strikes in the USA are the result of m
29. her saying it was probably just a matter of time, and he'd pointed out that she didn't have unlimited time and again s
30. Conway in his delightful book, The Crowd in Peace and War, points out that the crowd likes old men. In war, it chooses
31. achieved in nine months of digging at site 50, Glynn Isaac points out that 'the site has provided particularly clear e
32. rature of the Earth will drop with alarming rapidity. Hoyle points out that there was an abrupt change in surface condi
33. ed shellfish from the nearby rocky shore, and Richard Klein points out that 'this is the earliest evidence found anywhe
34. face towards each other. There was more leg-room there, she pointed out. The other passengers took elaborate pains not
35. any of her husbands. 'He stands to gain,' Tusker had often pointed out to Lucy. 'And he feeds her up a beat. One day s
36. es, but the garage is closed today. It's Easter Sunday.' He points out to Patrick that the steel door of the garage par
37. om Plato's myth - ' 'Whoa, hold it,' said Cantabile, and he pointed out to Polly: 'All you have to do is ask him a ques
38. ore than a few minutes every other day if we took turns,' I pointed out. 'Turns! Schedules! Lists! Did anyone ever tell
39. phasizing the harshness of the change. 'You see,' Stanitsyn pointed out, 'when Chekhov was first presented, the parts w
40. m. He hasn't got anyone to support. ' 'In any case,' Martin pointed out, 'you're my wife's parents, and how would I fee

promise

1. owledge the appropriateness of the medical treatment and to promise a change in his behaviour. Volpin felt that he had b
2. w what the purpose of the robberies was; they had each been promised a cut of the total, and being small fry had done wh
3. at the campus, prowling like a tiger. But at two sharp, as promised, Agrot rang; and at five past I was in the scroller
4. h 1970-71, he had traveled around the country for McGovern, promising a new world to the young, a world that would be fr
5. u do it? Tell me, at least.' Some other time, the professor promised, and took himself off. Peel's mind was full of othe
6. ew highways, new roads, new power plants, new schools. They promise better hospitals, housing, mental health centers, we
7. y What's-her-name. Just let me try. I won't take any risk - promise. Go on - go over there.' I did as she said and she s
8. aybe not - at his Fuhrer watching him. I won't fail you, he promised. He looked about - at the place where so much, so g
9. on't you - I mean, tell me?' She put a hand on his arm. Tom promised he would and then carefully recorded the two teleph
10. exander that Frederica had had too much to drink and he had promised her Alexander would take her home. Alexander said h
11. kes thin-armed teenagers look like flamingoes). Moreover, I promised her to throw a party at our house to which she woul
12. of words to spell, or a long mental arithmetic problem. He promised him a stamp album and a trip to the seaside if he p
13. office. 'Bill ... bill ... bill ... which I do not pay,' he promised himself. He brightened. There was a knock at the do
14. y when you've finished that, but don't let Jim get at it. I promised his mother not to let him drink himself to oblivion
15. 'Ah, don't be sentimental,' he said, smiling. 'I won't,' I promised. I was surprised to find it was only lunchtime - it
16. what the new doctors say,' Francois countered evasively. 'I promise I'll come to you when I feel I need help.' Mopani wa
17. slumbers, was the person least amused by the situation. He promised Joachim a good talking to. 'This,' he said, 'is not
18. ightpaths took a maddening forty minutes. (The brochure had promised: 'Just ten minutes from Kennedy.') It took another
19. as much as I enjoyed talking Danish.) I thanked him warmly, promised Jytte to be back for lunch, got my letters and pape
20. tituation the girl is likely to encounter. Magazine stories promise marriage with the boss, the colleges promise interes
21. hen her mother said, with great intensity, 'Ginny, you must promise me that you will put me out of my misery if I'm ever
22. harcoal trees and we knew that we'd played too long. We had promised Mother we would fetch some wood. We had to get some
23. ollywood movie. I don't go for that. I can't imagine myself promising my whole lifetime away. I might want to get marrie
24. ooks up, and stares, and says: 'My God, look at the time. I promised Myra I'd be home at seven to eat her steak. I can't
25. exaggerating for dramatic effect. All the same, I made her promise not to go out alone in the evenings. Then I went to
26. excusing both them and ourselves. 'Well, he is, Auntie! He promised not to tell!' 'OW!' My fingers itched to pull her b
27. e to lie to you very well,' he said 'I won't make a fuss, I promise.' 'Please understand that l am ready,' Barak said 'I
28. nt in: Plant when it is raining if you can, or when rain is promised. Put large plants in with a trowel and smaller ones
29. y well that suicide for him was out of the question. He had promised Sarah that one day they would be together again. He
30. repairs stated in the tenancy agreement. lf a landlord has promised that certain work will be done then he has right of
31. e without a producer now, I complained to Lew Grade and was promised that one would come soon. I would climb into the ca
32. was delicious.' 'We might be able to do better than that,' promised the colonel, searching carefully through the ranks
33. ther Al, who had just been drafted two weeks before. Al had promised to break every bone in Claude's body if he came bac
34. thing of that time. He still had a suit of the period, and promised to bring it to the office to show me. 'They knew ho
35. Mr Boylan and the head waiter. The head waiter disappeared, promising to call them when their table was ready. Mr Boylan
36. arted off. I was dropped off with the camels. Jan and David promised to come and pick us up in a week. I saddled up and
37.) I HAVE written before now about Sainsbury's and Waitrose, promising to deal from time to time with other supermarkets
38. ke for the next year's applications. She looked uneasy, but promised to follow his advice. The next time he saw her, she
39. just after eleven, giving me messages for them in Oxford. I promised to ring her that night, we'd have a whole evening t
40. age, and so on. I said I wasn't sure. He ended by making me promise to show him the gun before I paid hard cash for it.

prove, demonstrate, show

1   other reasons for women working. A national survey in 1968 proved that one-sixth of British wives work despite strong
2   o deal with them. Laboratory tests on men and animals alike prove that the more the choices, the slower the reaction ti
3   James Chadwick who broke with that deeply rooted idea, and proved in 1932 that the nucleus consists of two kinds of pa
4   the test period.) This Australian study took two years and proves that young people can be influenced to refrain from
5   ing about this object is its antiquity. Geological evidence proves beyond doubt that it is three million years old. It
6   later, we have the Industrial Relations Act. Yet the facts prove that industrial relations have altered little, except
7   y, the decisive British medical investigation which finally proved that smoking causes lung cancer was already being ca
8   sky, Floyd remembered how often his fellow scientists had 'proved' that interstellar travel was impossible. The journe
9   . Research at Durham, London and Edinburgh universities has proved that babies can locate sound, recognise their mother
10 ere clearly wrong. Subsequent studies, the world over, have proved conclusively that people place a far higher value on
11 rowded cities, but research by organisations like the NSPCC proves that facilities must be improved if children are goi
12 e keeps the candidate's nose to the grindstone. Our results prove that with bright pupils that is a fallacy. Under free
13 nes today. Descartes, one of the world's greatest thinkers, proved quite logically that the vacuum effects which Torric
14 world of sound is governed by exact numbers. He went on to prove that the same thing is true of the world of vision. T
15
16 tly on our fragile planet. The famous Harris survey of 1977 demonstrated, in its own words, that 'Significant majoritie
17 of Men and Families. Gaskell (1833) and Cobbett (1827) both demonstrate that there was certainly some long-range upward
18 n the animal kingdom that does not exist in reality, Darwin demonstrated that the driving force of evolution comes from
19 ways, we manage to stretch these limits, yet ample evidence demonstrates that our capabilities are finite. To discover
20 of survival'. In its conclusions it states 'This report has demonstrated that large numbers of old people in Islington
21 ically in more recent times. For instance, biochemists have demonstrated that the proteins that make up the bodies of h
22 d prepared his case thoroughly, Using charts and graphs, he demonstrated that known in-flight disasters caused by bombs
23 Lyme Regis in Persuasion). Getting into his stride, Morris demonstrated that Mr Elton was obviously implied to be impo
24 nts by Ross Ashby, H. D. Block, Frank Rosenblatt and others demonstrate that machines can learn from their mistakes, im
25 toxic chemicals. A report by Friends of the Earth recently demonstrated that the uncontrolled use of pesticides in Bri
26 that they were hopelessly convinced of my guilt. Our survey demonstrated that the majority of the people in Marin Count
27 y in comparison with renting. Some work has been done which demonstrates fairly conclusively that in English-speaking c
28
29 years, six years, twelve years.' And research with animals shows that males will mother an infant as well as any femal
30 ndependently of the preferences of other individuals. Arrow shows that with three alternatives (A, B and C) then: 1/3 o
31 at the expense of the rest of society. Research in Britain shows fairly conclusively that the welfare state does not r
32 tes, it did not stop the incidence of strikes. The evidence shows that it could well have had the reverse effect. If on
33 ians and professional memorizers for centuries. Experiments showed that by using these systems anyone could remember un
34 half. An opinion poll released by the Allensbach institute shows 'that 62% of West Germans 'greatly desire' reunificati
35 went to bed hungry. The noted economist Colin Clark later showed that Boyd-Orr's successors knew this statement was u
36 there.' The House and Commons Expenditure Committee report showed that three quarters of the jobs go to boys, with gir
37 tion pattern of the poor. They suggested that their results showed that 'low income groups and large families tend to b
38 lion sales its obvious everyone reads them. A recent survey showed that my books sold well in Boston which considers it
39 1976/7. Although this is a significant reduction, the table shows that most of this redistribution took place before th
40 ays, so did additional traffic arrive to fill it up. Webber shows conclusively that 'BART has brought about a rise in t

put it

1. ne up an assistant. To help in his research, was the way he put it.' 'A woman?' 'He said a person.' Gaspar says, 'Patri
2. t be raised. An interim arrangement, yes, that's the way to put it. An interim arrangement to help Sahib recover his ow
3. and. He was sad that I was leaving for 'so far away', as he put it, and made ne promise to write to him from time to ti
4. es or drastically disturbing the neighbours,' as one member put it. Another said, 'It's a middle-aged person's response
5. s are never successes in the ordinary sense of the word. To put it another way, they never make money. In fact they rar
6. for as long as white men have ruled the world. The Africans put it another way: When the white man came to Africa, the
7. ty of churches of Wren. But Renaissance? John Summerson has put it best: 'Paul van Somer, whose portraits hang happily
8. ugh to make him a desirable acquisition for an employer. To put it bluntly, people like him were two a penny. Why did h
9. to higher-level jobs themselves. As Westergaard and Resler put it: 'But to say that circulation is fluid is not to say
10. uld have taken the ultimate risk. He was, as Sarah had once put it, 'going too far'. At two o'clock in the morning Cast
11. raphs of her you feel she's one of the family.' As the song puts it, 'I know that we have met before and danced before,
12. of its emotional origins as we require it to be in men'. To put it in more general terms: man is moral, woman amoral, m
13. inks it is his. She may feel like a nobody, but the way she puts it is: 'Oh, I'm very happy, but I wish George were bet
14. e ways of love. 'Letting go' is perhaps a friendlier way to put it. It implies generosity, a talent a good mother needs
15. more serious musical figure of the Sixties, Pierre Boulez, put it like this: 'Purely thematic writing has no future. I
16. ing the same mass values. Duane Elgin, the American author, puts it like this: 'We have inadvertently handed over a sub
17. e came as a considerable surprise. West Yellowstone was, to put it mildly, unlike any other town on earth. To begin wit
18. nnel officer at the London HQ of a large industrial company put it precisely: 'Let's face it, after you've been a secre
19. s to make money for the shareholders and not as one manager put it 'run a holiday camp for the workers'. Some employers
20. critical revision give rise to new problems (P2). As Popper puts it, 'science begins with problems and ends with proble
21. er father committed.' 'There again one had to - how shall I put it - step backwards instead of forward,' said Poirot. '
22. o give confidence where a woman needs it, as the TV adverts put it. Still, Sally had said she owed it to herself as a f
23. do many things, but do we know what to do? Ortega y Gasset put it succinctly: 'We cannot live on the human level witho
24. he pleasure of a visit from you?' 'It's very nice of you to put it that way,' said Mrs Oliver. 'I don't know that it wi
25. ing to the Ball together; 'as a little party', Margaret had put it. The second thing Dixon knew and Mar- garet didn't w
26. xperience and hope for. A feminist photographer, Jo Spence, put it this way: 'What we need to do with our own pictures
27. main block. lt was intended, as a contemporary description put it, 'to accommodate any guest, who may find inconvenien
28. around, and that therefore she was showing off. As one boy put it to her, 'You are just a silly little goose. You swea
29. , some weeks and several letters to both of them later, she put it to him that she was bothered about Olive's approach.
30. ugh, had his own instinctive measure of time. He was, as he put it to himself, 'sick and tired' of having matters of wh
31. slightly irregular teeth. Then he cheered up a little as he put it to himself that her attachment to Bertrand was a fai
32. at meet merely once a week, after work time. As Philip once put it to me, in these conditions 'You're not really at you
33. very court. That, they insist, is both fair and biblical. I put it to Nick Miller, when I met him, that it might be Old
34. ame to re-examine. 'You said to Mr Fairbairn - or rather he put it to you - that Griffiths was driving round the public
35. n Report. The discussion at this meeting was, as one member put it, 'very lively'. The rumours in the press were having
36. derful than the wildest fantasy. The great J. B. S. Haldane put it very well when he said: 'The universe is not only qu
37. gged on the floor in caftans and believed that, as Mr Stamp put it, 'We are, literally, what we eat.' At the back of mu
38. than to the long term, because in the long term, as Keynes put it with cheerful brutality, we are all dead. And then,
39. atrolling of the corridors, to keep an eye on things, as he put it, with deliberate vagueness, to himself. One day as h
40. s resounding defeat at Kip's Bay and fled (or as Washington put it 'withdrew') to the village of Haarlem. With two juni

remind

1 nomadic pastoral society, that of the Boers, who, as we are reminded, differed in their cultural equipment from the Zul
2 ars being boiled alive like lobsters!' Miss Jackson, when I reminded her about the copper, said that her mind was so en
3 der the bed for her shoes. 'Your car is miles away,' Stuart reminded her. 'Don't worry about me,' she said tartly. 'I'm
4 ipped. But I caught her wrists easily and held her down and reminded her she was only seventeen and very beautiful, tha
5 For the Fatherland.' 'And I'm sure you were aware,' Fassler reminded her, 'that if you didn't cooperate, he could have
6 is mother said. 'It's a fine name.' Thomas didn't bother to remind her that the boy's name was Wesley Jordache, nor did
7 hing she could do. She arranged to phone the Fox officer to remind her to wake me, but I think she also saw to it that
8 fought to dispel her own depression about Jane's illness by reminding herself how much worse it could have been (Jane's
9 s and its effect on him was almost invariably negative. She reminded herself to make sure to apply for absentee ballots
10 k in the Smokies. But at least she still rode planes, Ginny reminded herself - unlike her mother, who in recent years h
11 wanted him in bed. 'Eight sharp, and no stay of execution. Remind him about the gymkhana the day after tomorrow, for w
12 e of instincts.' 'Of which the quest for meaning is one,' I reminded him, finger aloft. 'It's a hunt for a unicorn,' he
13 was on his own. 'What seems to be the trouble?' he asked. I reminded him of my earlier visit, 'Ah, yes,' he told me. 'I
14 Meehan's call to Stranraer Police Station on Sunday 6th to remind him of the name of the garage; Allan Burgess, son of
15 me,' he said. 'Tomorrow will be quite suitable.' Miss Lemon reminded him of two appointments which he already had, but
16 d I'll bet you pestered him about those old times.' 'Yes, I reminded him.' 'You would. And I suppose it was disagreeabl
17 a greater stratagem than his ill-timed knowingness, and he reminded himself that you could not be too careful. 'Where
18 e to contact a professional who knew his job thoroughly. He reminded himself to thank Louis appropriately - after the j
19 ight, by that time, have. But if there were no wreckage, he reminded himself, what could they prove? Nothing! The fligh
20 lady cried, 'Labels! Now really, Alexandra, you should have reminded me. I'm afraid you've got into a lot of this mess
21 ere's no reason to shout. You're the one that's deaf,' Hugo reminded me rudely. 'Let's forget the slums for a moment,'
22 ing security so lightly. Kendra and Franklin Alexander kept reminding me that if anything ever happened to me they woul
23 . And began lying low. But then Sabine von Planta called to remind me that we had pre-arranged a date for that evening
24 with a few comrades from the area. I accepted, and someone reminded me that we must hurry to meet my mother's plane. I
25 e ended up admonishing each other for the same reasons. She reminded me this time to eat more and try to gain my own we
26 me to any harm either, and that I never came back. She also reminded me to be careful, as I was still under a suspended
27 king of sending me abroad again by any chance?' 'No. Why?' 'Remind me to speak to you about Davis.' The light turned gr
28 o us there. When our children are about to go to school, we remind ourselves of what it was like for us, and we are oft
29 tremendous advertising campaign was mounted: consumers were reminded that no real lady or gentleman was ever seen in pu
30 all aware that we had together made history in that room. I reminded the senators of this and of their duty to preserve
31 rch of a watch. 'Changing, we were told,' the military lady reminded them. 'If you ask me, she bloody well forgot she w
32 avoid two lost years in the Army. I've written to the CIA, reminding them of my meeting with Gus, and asking to be rec
33 refill their cups. Sloan had been glancing at his watch and reminding them that he had to clean up the house. They had
34 g discomfort, you should complain to your local council and remind them that they should enforce this Act. If people co
35 'll fetch Miss Winter now. The lady from Wolverhampton,' he reminded us, as he set off across the hall again. Miss Wint
36 is good for him must be good for all men. Joseph Collignon reminds us, however, that there is a reverse of the coin: M
37 us most of the main groups in poverty, but as Steve Winyard reminds us, it is important to make a distinction between t
38 ad. 'There are worse things than illness,' Dr. Holmes wryly reminds us. 'No one can live without experiencing some degr
39 hich malnutrition stultifies the brain, in which, as Hobbes reminded us, the typical life is 'poor, nasty, brutish, and
40 home there will be speaking bathroom scales, freezers which remind you to restock them, cookers which tell you how the

shout, cry, exclaim, mutter, scream, whisper, yell

1 d come out. Then she scarcely glanced at the poor man; just shouted at him for spoiling her lovely evening. If that's n
2 ing. 'Time, gentlemen, Please.' 'There are ladies present!' shouted Daisy, banging her glass on the table. She shouted
3 ket there was an uproar in the audience. A local politician shouted: 'Don't drag politics into sport!' and one of the S
4 owing stones and pebbles at the door. 'Get out of here,' he shouted. 'Get out of here at once,' and his face was so red
5   two sharp cracks, one quickly after the other, and a voice shouted: 'Keep still, woman! Hold that accursed horse quiet
6 nsciousness and suffocating. 'For God's sake, let me down,' shouted Mary. 'Hang on, we'll have a go at pulling you up,'
7 aw that they were in danger of being surrounded. Frederick shouted to his men to get out while the going was good, and
8
9 ts hung from the banisters. 'You wouldn't believe it,' Mary cried. 'Ellen got them from the Esso Service Station. Georg
10 e were drowned in the depth of the sea.' 'Oh, Tony, don't!' cried Karin, so sharply that we both jumped. 'Sorryl' said
11 as startled by the fevered look of his patient. When Robert cried out 'Did you listen to her heart?' he spoke calmly as
12 it was all wonderful, wonderful. 'You're marvellous !' she cried out to the actors, feeling as if her powerfully criti
13 and lifted the baby up off the mother's lap. 'Good God!' he cried. 'She weighs a ton!.' 'Exactly.' 'Now isn't that marv
14
15 the secret news?' 'I'm getting married.' 'Married!' Daintry exclaimed. 'Does your mother know?' 'I've just said that I
16 e pleased as he listened. 'Best news I've heard this year!' exclaimed the doctor delightedly. 'It solves a lot of my pr
17 r-struck. 'Do you know how much those things are worth?' he exclaimed. 'Thousands! Some of them are collector's items.
18 al right to decline a summons. The doctor's response was to exclaim: 'What's all this nonsense! If you refuse to come t
19
20 g nervous, and Don Albino was visibly losing confidence. He muttered about it being a long time since he had walked int
21 the thing in utter disgust. 'I don't know what to say,' he muttered. 'It's all so awful.' 'You can say that again,' th
22 Mr Hughes's voice, issuing from the darkness, was heard to mutter that I was trying to sabotage the meeting. When ligh
23 g was and where, grave, thy victory. 'As if I bloody knew,' muttered the Vicar and reached for the whisky bottle only t
24
25 ds ahead, I was just about to call to her when suddenly she screamed, 'Alan! Alan! ' in obvious terror. I was alongside
26 s any more. I do as I'm told.' 'Where's a doctor?' his wife screamed. 'He's on his way! ' someone called from the door.
27 omintang broke into her home and tried to take me away. She screamed that I was her daughter. She didn't even know who
28 'Do you confess that you stole these things?' 'No, no, no!' screamed the boy. 'It is a mistake. I swear on the soul of
29
30 ly around the perimeter of the clearing. 'Follow me,' Claud whispered. 'And keep down.' He started crawling away swiftl
31 tention and had no notion of what to do. In desperation she whispered in my ear that there was a toilet in the back and
32 wondered what it could be. 'It's your Uncle Ray come home,' whispered Mother. 'Get up now and let him sleep.' I saw a r
33 nately. I've tried everything else.' 'Who are they?' Sheila whispered to Adam. 'Actors.' 'She fancies me,' Denis said,
34
35 stairs to the car at the kerbside. 'Back to the office,' he yelled at the driver. In the telephone booth in the foyer o
36 me an easy grin. I managed the weakest of weak smiles, and yelled down to Robin to hurry up. But by the time he reache
37 e of his head ended the sentence. 'Keep your hands off me,' yelled Eva, and putting her knowledge of Judo to good use h
38 father's house and let himself inside with his own key. He yelled out, 'Ma, where are you?' and his mother came out of
39 ulp magazine I had borrowed the other day. From her room Lo yelled she had it. We are quite a lending library in this h
40 ou find Marion.' I whirled around and raced off. 'Wait!' he yelled. 'What's your name?' I didn't answer. I was gasping

so, not

1. ass us among our followers?' he asked. 'No, I don't believe so,' I replied. 'Try it and see. I'm certain the reaction w
2. hing. 'What's the rent? Is it to rent?' I asked. 'I believe so, though we could inquire. Of course it would be better i
3. r! A chap gets sharp set out in the air all day.' 'I expect so,' said Hilary, gazing at him fondly through her thick sp
4. w from you, is that what you want? ' Jules smiled. 'I guess so. But you don't know the medical setup. Whatever you may
5. anything. Are you recovered from your cold? I heartily hope so. If you have nothing better to do I advise you to go and
6. their permission.' 'Perhaps it'll be a girl.' 'God, I hope so,' Adam said. 'Otherwise ... OK, it's ridiculous but I re
7. really under there?' said my sister, and Amy said she hoped so. 'As long as I know where he is, it doesn't feel so dang
8. ile. 'I should say they've got a lot in common.' 'I imagine so.' A maidservant was now collecting the used crockery, an
9. or she'd have been unconscious by now?' - I should imagine so.' I pushed back my chair. 'She'll be asleep in fifteen m
10. ongratulated today, too, I take it.' Boylan said. 'I reckon so. At least, that's the theory.' Brad grinned. 'We'll need
11. ia. And the heat; June - the worst month, everyone had said so. But the Temple was magnificent - and the afternoon was
12. ilence. Mr Hendriks obviously didn't like the idea. He said so, but obliquely: 'What you are saying, Mister S., is that
13. etter. He'd like to know you better. He likes you - he said so. And, no, we weren't discussing you - your name cropped
14. id, 'be serious.' 'No,' he said. 'Why not.' 'Because I said so. Be careful, you're going to get flour all over that cle
15. . What do you mean, you don't believe it?' I said. 'It says so on the news.' I could feel myself getting all hot under
16. I happen to think you've done an incompetent job. I've said so in my report.' 'I thought it was a committee report not
17. ' 'And are you on speaking terms with them now?' 'I suppose so.' 'Good.' She sighed and poured herself another cup of t
18. would have to get another teacher in my place.' 'I suppose so,' I agreed. For one dreadful minute my old doubts return
19. thers want to know, don't you think?' 'Well, yes, I suppose so, but after all they don't really matter -' 'Not as much
20. ou know, chief bridesmaid and all that?' 'No, I don't think so. If I do, I'll let you know.' 'But shouldn't a bride be
21. ther. My novel will make some money. I know you don't think so! Only I can't write at present, I try every day but I ju
22. ?' 'Give it to me.' 'Can you do it with one hand?' 'I think so.' 'If not I could do it for you.' 'Let me try.' Flecker
23. ind too. Did you miss me?' 'I think so,' said Tim. 'I think so! That's a fine Tim Reedeish remark! So it's over?' 'What
24. ds a bit of a nuisance to me,' said Rose, who did not think so, but expected Miss Lindey to think so. 'She's not really
25. . 'So I live quite well. Though some people might not think so.' He had tried hard to follow this, while she was speaki
26. ttracts you most?' I wanted to get up and leave. I told him so. 'Stay here and talk like a man,' he said. As only the s
27. n the way I was to set about it. I knew, for he had told me so, that she was frightened of the violence she encounters
28. istakes.' 'Your whole life's a mistake. You've just told me so.' 'All the more reason for not dragging you into it.' 'I
29. ate they'll all have the satisfaction of saying 'I told you so'. Terror was depriving Tim of his wits and he could not
30.
31. om her shopping yet?' demanded Fanny. 'No, ma'am, I believe not.' Fanny found the old lady's condition so dismal that s
32. t pocket.) Would Anne be with her? The Count ardently hoped not. The Count had written (briefly, soberly) to say that h
33. he said to Gretchen. 'Do you think it's possible?' 'I hope not,' Gretchen said. 'What's all this about?' Johnny answer
34. d if she would run for the U.S. Senate, he replied, 'I hope not.' Aides say that Reagan regretted the remark and that h
35. n my way.' 'You haven't lost the ticket, have you?' 'I hope not,' he said, feeling in his waistcoat pocket. 'No, here i
36. .' ' It doesn't often happen,' Castle said. ' No, I suppose not.' 'You see, my wife's nervous when she's left alone in
37. your cabin.' 'Oh, no! We couldn't do that.' 'No, I suppose not.' I tried to think why not, but I was too old. I couldn
38. she began to repair her make-up. ' No, I don't.' 'I thought not,' she said between peerings and puffs and dabs. When sh
39. Hall ... 'You're fired!' he shouted. Wilt smiled. 'I think not,' he said. 'Here are my terms ...' 'Your what?' 'My ter
40. story about it.' 'I don't - I mean - ' 'I should just think not! But you mustn't get all mixed up about Gertrude. She's

suggest

1   e and accusing. Some were very long indeed. In none did she suggest a meeting or hint at a pardon. She eventually decid
2   t having a reaction from Mr Mawne's perfidious attentions?' suggested Amy. 'Is this the brave front put on by an unfulf
3   could be set up in the Middle East. Such a zone, Mr Rostow suggested, could be based on the one set up by the Treaty o
4   ed it to her mother. 'Let me walk you to your car,' Joe Bob suggested gallantly as Ginny was leaving. Just then the doo
5   nd behaviour problems than girls. Several reasons have been suggested, genetic and environmental. J. M. Tanner showed t
6   g. It was the Colonel's wife, the night before, who quietly suggested: 'I do think pheasant shooting is a bit cruel. Af
7   here should be something on the top of the Flat Iron,' John suggested. 'I'll have a look,' said Dougal, always ready to
8   n fitness tests along the way to monitor their progress. He suggested I try it and I went out on my first run in the pr
9   he previous fortnight on a diet of pasta and plain bread. I suggested inviting Denny, and Jim agreed. We brought him up
10 rability, of the economy of that country. 'Viability', they suggest, is not a 'purely' economic concept; 'purely' econo
11 its mind more on the game than the million. Six figures, I suggest, is some sort of turning point in the career, and t
12 ly had never been used for cutting anything. The reason, he suggests, is that it was meant for 'higher' purposes. Engra
13 ientists. An application for one bacterium has already been suggested. It could be used to mop up the waste hydrogen wh
14 eep going: and Lionel was a kind man. 'Let me make it,' she suggested. 'It'll give me something to do while everybody g
15 rogue to earn his eternal approval. 'Meet me here at 8.30,' suggested Kleiber. 'It will give you time for your preening
16 his had been an excuse in case he found me tiresome. He had suggested meeting in the park because it would be easy to l
17   both, and cheerful company. Perhaps one of her sisters, he suggested, might be summoned, to be with her for a few week
18 . The Chinese American astronomer Hong-Yee Chiu (1932-) has suggested one interesting explanation. The nuclear reaction
19 be that there is an Englishman who does this kind of work,' suggested one of the inspectors. 'But he's not on our file
20 ing was wet and soggy. We put up the tent and had a brew. I suggested rather tentatively that we went up and had a try
21 ek, Mrs Castle.' (There had been a time when Mrs Castle had suggested Sarah should call her ' mother ', but she had bee
22 eer vandalism and senseless behaviour. Young people, he   suggested, should try to find employment by showing tha
23 competitively on the world market free of all subsidies. We suggest that all such subsidies be phased out over a period
24 son Martin confided in me that he intended to escape, and I suggested that he wait until I was released; I would assist
25 for a long time, said that I looked a bit peaky to him, and suggested that I had a 'glass of stout and something substa
26 dent in France. I told him it had also been an accident. He suggested that I turn myself in. He also suggested I consul
27 r that she had a spider on her leg. As I expected, Patricia suggested that Kaspar should try to hypnotise me. He preten
28 on's idea of relaxation, and, secondly, it is ridiculous to suggest that life in modern cities is more stressful than l
29   B.C. Diogenes of Apollonia advanced a different theory. He suggested that memory was a process which consisted of even
30   than a year. Chesterton took numerous members with him but suggested that others remain as otherwise it would be 'impo
31   began Strachey took me aside to 'explain the position'. He suggested that the game should be played, 'for obvious reas
32 'patience, sisters,' and closed her eyes. Meanwhile someone suggested that they break into small groups to discuss how
33 n he also has the right to sell an old state.' 'Perhaps,' I suggested, 'the Canadians would be so good as to buy your o
34 t for a new hat.' 'What about the one with the cherries?' I suggested. The hat with the cherries is an old and valued f
35   the Notting Hill newspaper Frendz. At the third meeting we suggested the idea of producing an alternative magazine for
36 erican Constitution. When the name of George Washington was suggested to him, to help him fix his generation, he said h
37 Nancy Ryan said she wouldn't mind striding the streets, and suggested to me that we escape the confusion in the lobby b
38 g to his father so that the father could not return home. I suggested to the father that he stay for a few days. I had
39 ted, and let Aida herself go hang. After the performance, I suggested we go eat at a pizza parlor. 'Well, pizza is quic
40 ry said. 'I've forgotten his name.' 'Watson?' the brigadier suggested. 'Yes, Watson.' 'So you've even been checking our

threaten

1. his two brothers, who jointly owned the house with him and threatened a lawsuit. 'I'm thinking of building a hotel on
2. ot a violent person, but I did once, and totally seriously, threaten a woman that, if she pushed in front of me again,
3. young lady found her lover was unfaithful, and pined away - threatening before she died to come and claim the fickle ma
4. sed woman, and reproved Darrell for his part in the affair, threatening him with imprisonment if he did anything of the
5. rd wrongly or doesn't always want to read. Above all, don't threaten him with school, or emphasize unduly the part that
6. y off me, or I might.' 'Don't threaten me, Ginny.' 'I'm not threatening, I'm just warning,' 'And I'm warning you.' 'Wel
7. need the anchor a bit more.' 'I have this feeling I'm being threatened.' 'It could be. It could be that the most import
8. . For Humboldt was litigious. The word was made for him. He threatened many times to sue me. Yes, the obituary was awfu
9. nstead, my mother protected me from the world and my father threatened me with it. My feeling of inadequacy increased s
10. lly trying, even though she wants to and thinks she is. She threatens or scolds or punishes frequently. But one such mo
11. ger on Wendy and me and the children. They stepped up their threatening phone calls, which usually came at about three
12. with your job anyway and the event which has caused you to threaten resignation has merely acted as a trigger. If you
13. ience, and the events which follow the announcement of your threatened resignation will give invaluable insight into th
14. aggressive to the point of being dangerous. At one point he threatens Socrates with violence. Phaedrus, in Greek, means
15. uri Daniel; a Russian representative visited the B.B.C. and threatened that Russian co-operation in B.B.C. enterprises
16. , which is to be held on neutral territory, but the new UAR threatens that there could be immediate military action aga
17. owing way. Suppose that the Russians are at the Channel and threaten that, unless Britain surrenders, they will begin b
18. s from everyone, and there were notices in the barrack huts threatening the death sentence for anyone not handing his c
19. was. If there was going to be a power-cut tomorrow, as was threatened, then it would be sensible to get a camper's sto
20. t into a slanging-match with the station commander until he threatened to arrest me for 'disturbing the peace, using ab
21. e, all that I cancelled and cursed. You may jeer at me, and threaten to clear the court, but until I am gagged and half
22. f indignation from Jefferson's partisans. The Chief Justice threatened to clear the court of spectators. For several da
23. one. During the afternoon he suddenly remembered Loebel had threatened to come, at a precise hour, bringing an American
24. o have held one of his leading ladies out of the window and threatened to drop her if she did not sing in tune. He rema
25. was that when Charles Lee was captured by the British, they threatened to hang him for a deserter from the British army
26. o had seduced her son. The father became almost violent and threatened to have Paul put in prison. 'I'll ruin you, I'll
27. e very least a kindly pat on the head. My father was always threatening to horsewhip his bank manager, but there's not
28. er.' She stopped. 'And then?' 'I let him in the door and he threatens to kill me if I don't do what he wants.' 'Does he
29. m, she knows the real money power is with him. When the man threatens to leave her, instead of quickly thinking of ways
30. he Frenchman's face had turned bright-red, and he furiously threatened to lock us all up for five years and throw the b
31. e appeared. She wondered if he intended to beat her; he had threatened to once or twice previously, but her preg- nancy
32. stion for a long time, and eventually he only agreed when I threatened to resign. Much as I liked and admired Frank, I
33. that, if it would be more effective if Britain itself could threaten to retaliate, and the objection to this is only th
34. be expected to do so; Mr Brooke actually went so far as to threaten to return the money to the bank, though not quite
35. day, Atkins, the manager, tried to slide out of it, so they threatened to strike next morning. He paid up at once. A Su
36. serted as it appeared, a notice at the gate of a side-track threatened TRESPASSERS WILL BE SHOT AT ON SIGHT. TRY IT AND
37. ng the Foreign Secretary under a hypnotic influence. He was threatened with assault in the street and was in some dange
38. NAACP was declared illegal in Alabama, and its members were threatened with imprisonment. My parents were both members
39. the main gate. I never did get put on report, though I was threatened with it twice - once for going across to the hos
40. and once to the military-registration office, where he was threatened with the loss of his pension if he did not curta

warn

1. stry will have no alternative but to raise our rates.' But, warns a government official, 'that would damage the whole i
2. love improves adults. Small children who are always sternly warned against getting their clothes dirty or making a mess
3. class warfare had no relevance to the Kenyan situation, and warned against 'more subtle' forms of imperialism, Western
4. response to the EEC bid was chilly, and one representative warned Brussels not to try 'divide and conquer' tactics. Th
5. boating at Maidenhead?' 'Not too much excitement,' Clarissa warned from the doorway. 'Oh go away,' Etta said. 'Let Jump
6. er own. She was mildly objecting to this when I appeared. I warned her about talking to strange men but she insisted th
7. nd fanned herself with them. 'Be careful with that,' Sudhir warned her. 'It's our report on 'Cultural Trends - East and
8. Sylvia until she became old enough to get away from home. I warned her that there was a danger that she might marry the
9. in the van as one of the policemen took Mr Webster aside to warn him about his son. Mrs Webster leaned against the door
10. u of course, for instance I wasn't sure how carefully you'd warned him about talking to strangers and so on - if you ha
11. ered a French plane and filled it with equipment. The pilot warned him it was overloaded and wouldn't fly. Like Sir Pat
12. , and when I was appointed to the cabinet I went to him and warned him. Lewis, I said, get out of the country. Take you
13. freely of the desirability of separating west from east. I warned him not to give a wrong impression of what we were a
14. n by Northcliffe himself for the issue of 21 May. His staff warned him of the possible consequences, including imprison
15. rth that year.1 His friend and adviser, Frederick T. Gates, warned him of the terrible danger he faced: Your fortune is
16. ace was in darkness. Griffiths crossed the road, and Meehan warned him to be careful of the dog. There were now only a
17. He lurched unsteadily towards the door. 'Don't you go out!' warned his mother. 'There's plenty for you to do here, and
18. scrub that plummeted towards the plain. 'Do not look down,' warned Koda Dad. 'Look up!' Ash jerked his gaze from the gu
19. satisfy me. Finally he unlocked the door of a room that, he warned me, cost more than any of the others; decorated in s
20. m pressed, but I can probably avoid giving explanations, He warned me, however, not to tell anyone that I am going to O
21. r a long time? Was leaving the convent part of it too? They warned me that it would be worse, that I would collapse lat
22. omantic' to go to such a place. He shook his head at me and warned me to avoid it in future. Suddenly, he fired at me:
23. nly half the calories.' But across the aisle, Mrs. Gershwin warned Miss Putnam not to ruin her appetite by eating it. '
24. you have plenty of time, Madam' the butler said kindly. 'I warned Mr Foster that you must leave at nine-fifteen. There
25. rls watch the boys or play with dolls. Girls are commonly warned not to climb into trees or on to garage roofs becaus
26. aterials it may be dangerous to wear. Mothers are now being warned off children's pyjamas that are treated for fire-pro
27. pain - with 4.5 million acres of vineyards - joins the EEC. Warns one EEC official: 'We're seeing the first skirmishes
28. less prominent than white. 'Wait until you're thirty,' she warned. She might as well have told me to wait until I was
29. tor had prescribed for her stomach cramps, and she had been warned that it was dangerous to exceed the stated dose—one
30. hat they could eradicate the Medfly eventually, though they warned that spraying might continue through the winter and
31. n at a very isolated siding. Although the refugees had been warned that they would be met by men wearing British unifor
32. a stronger and more efficient legislature; and in debate he warned: 'The Parliamentary system is on trial ... I do not
33. cle of torchlight. 'Mm,' the fat man said after a while. 'I warned them at the Center about this.' There was a note of
34. ntent of the scene. In Scene 4 Charles stops the actors and warns them that it's coming out too conventional. The key t
35. calling a nurse whom he had taken out before: she had been warned to notify the police, and when he walked into her ap
36. find a guide for our trip. 'But it might be difficult,' he warned us. 'Everyone here is frightened of the volcano, and
37. special kinds of cigarettes, then the writing on the packet warns us that smoking damages our health. We read advertise
38. here ' The boys stood up. Tom smiled up at the soldier. 'I warned you.' he said. 'I'll be waiting for you outside.' 'G
39. got Mike wrong. You're mad because he lied to you. Well, he warned you never to ask him about business. You're mad beca
40. tarts asking you any questions,' said Lord Grant, 'I should warn you that you are not bound to answer any question the

wish

1. s watching us from the stairwell and the porch behind us. I wished Andy were here, but he must have gone straight back
2. 'Rudy!' Her pleasure at hearing his voice was a rebuke. He wished Boylan were not in the room. 'Julie,' he said, 'abou
3. the sparkling Christmas tree, we all sang carols together, wished each other a Merry Christmas, and went out into the
4. ach other as they ran up the road. We stood and sang grace, wished each other 'Good afternoon' and made our way into th
5. s, nearly hairless after years of chafing in long pants: He wished Ellen had come with him to make him feel less conspi
6. for walks and 'a breath of air'. Although I hated it all, I wished for it not to end, for I knew that with the end of s
7. e, try to look upon it as a life-enriching bonus. If you've wished for more time in the past - now's your time to use i
8. be a good chance that she could really help him. But merely wishing for relations to improve was taking something of a
9. light's good in Anne's room. But it isn't big enough.' Tim wished Gertrude would stop calling it 'Anne's room'. It was
10. flat. Now what the hell are you doing to it?' The inspector wished he carried a gun. 'All right,' he said quietly, wari
11. l and often felt jealous because David could go out when he wished - he even traveled back to Chicago. I stayed in, rea
12. him till that moment and now he simply hadn't the money. He wished he hadn't spent so much on Aurelia. There was the sc
13. t on their coats. He kissed Lili, shook hands with Alix and wished her a happy vacation, patted Max on the back. When h
14. swept away. The men were happy to say 'hello'. Many of them wished him good luck. One or two stood aside for a word whe
15. pped violently through the pages in search of something she wished Humbert to see. Found it at last. I faked interest b
16. He left me at the door of the Foremaster and for a moment I wished I could go with him. I thought home might be a mess.
17. sk they are less compassionate and wise than opinionated. I wish I could offer a magic solution to your problem. There
18. y alert. I felt scared, and a bit mad at being stared at. I wished I'd never come. 'Mary, can I say something very, ver
19. ' 'I see. I wish you hadn't told me. I'm not a talker but I wish I didn't know.' 'For that matter, I wish the same thin
20. Beetle and Wedge.' 'Bit big, aren't they?' I said, and then wished I hadn't. 'They says as he's settling down here,' sa
21. uch more exciting place to inhabit. I can see now he always wished I was older; it was as if he foresaw that when the n
22. for about that long. He is here to see we do the work as he wishes it done. Some actors suck up to the master, follow h
23. ed to remain close to his son by taking unpaid leave and he wishes it were possible to work a six-hour day, another Swe
24. fide to you a secret I have told to no living man.' 'Do you wish me to leave you, Cousin?' asked the Cardinal. 'No, I t
25. rich American. She kissed her hand as she waved goodbye and wished me well in the career that I was beginning, just as
26. d in a search for - -criminals, shall we say? Of course, we wished merely to eliminate you from our inquiries. You are
27. ineffable touch of winds. Suddenly she missed the wind and wished she could hear it blow. 'You cheer me up,' she said.
28. b smells came wafting, of jasmine and passion flowers. Judy wished she didn't have to go in again. Inside Mrs. Kaul was
29. ateurs - and proud of it. There were some days when Johnnie wished that he was working for the Americans. He had more i
30. sampled it and licked the red juice from her upper lip and wished that she were meeting the violinist for the first ti
31. ughout the meal. Among other things. He wished it was over, wished the whole visit over. He thought of the country cott
32. or. Gertrude and the Count sat hunched up over their cognac wishing they had brought their coats. Anne arrived. She had
33. r who was in labor with twins. At first the husband had not wished to allow his wife to come near the hospital, but, as
34. n her room in the flat in Burke Street, where her colleague wished to chat when she came in at night, and offered tea a
35. -normalize' the world around him by artificial means. If he wishes to improve his height, he can wear high-heeled shoes
36. ats back but also could beat the wife and divorce her if he wished to. In the rains since Kunta had returned from manho
37. on. But then she was in love with him, and so of course she wished to marry him; though perhaps not too soon. It would
38. sense of the word, Ladies. You had only to listen to Katie wishing us all 'Good evening and welcome' in Bulgarian to f
39. ound my waist, and didn't look at anyone or say anything. I wished we were alone, but we were not, and I had to talk to
40. something about it.' Stok and Vulkan exchanged glances. `I wish you would try to understand,' said Stok. `I am really

Answers to Exercises

Exercise 1
1. in a cafe (ordering something to eat and drink)
2. in a courtroom during a legal trial (<u>judge</u>, <u>jurors</u>)
3. in a rented flat or apartment (<u>landlord</u>, <u>vacate</u>)
4. on an aircraft (<u>captain</u>, <u>engine</u>)
5. in a war, or perhaps in a prison (<u>guards</u>, some people didn't get to their feet - perhaps they had died during the night)

Exercise 2
2. 'It would explode,' she claimed hopefully. (quote structure)
3. Denis claims it to be 20. (claim followed by noun group and 'to'- infinitive clause)
4. the pilots claimed not to feel anxious or worried (claim followed by 'to'- infinitive clause)
5. he never claimed to be an expert on virus diseases such as colds (claim followed by 'to'-infinitive clause)
6. few, Downs claims, would abolish bureaucracy if given the chance. (indirect report structure with the reporting clause in the middle)

Exercise 3
2. that 'anyone could act in the movies' or that 'dipl (a second 'that'-clause, very difficult to guess what is missing because even the subject is incomplete)
3. that Mars was covered with a spider's web of fine li (a 'that'-clause, almost complete - the last word is certainly <u>lines</u> and it completes the structure)
4. Were he to decrease them, he claimed, he would have to lower his standard of living drast (an indirect report structure with the reporting clause in the middle, almost complete - the last word must be <u>drastically</u> and it could complete the structure)
5. St. Mary has been claimed as the 'earliest true Gothic Revival church in London (a passive structure corresponding to 'claim a thing as something', almost complete - the last word is <u>London</u> and it could complete the structure)
6. questing, driven, thought-dominated man of the West, they claim (an indirect report structure with the reporting clause at the end - it is difficult to guess what the first part of the structure is, but it might be about what a certain person or kind of person is not, contrasting with the following sentence saying what he is).

Exercise 4
11. is most similar to 1 and 2 above, although 'that' is not used when the reporting clause comes in the middle of the reported clause
12. is also similar to 1 and 2 ('Gertrude admitted that she scarcely knew the art galleries')
13. is similar to 8 and 9 ('He admits to being a certain age, but he seems younger')
14. is a different and less common structure - 'admit something to be something'. Therefore, so far you have identified 5 main structures for admit, plus 1 less common one:
    a. 'that'-clause
    b. quote
    c. '-ing' clause
    d. preposition 'to'
    e. noun group
    f. noun group + 'to'-infinitive clause

Exercise 5
1. speaker: my father; hearer: me
2. hearer: he (no speaker)
3. speaker: I (no hearer)
4. (no speaker or hearer)

When **threaten** is followed by a prepositional phrase with 'with', you mention the hearer; you can mention the speaker (1) or avoid this by using a passive (2). In other structures (e.g. when **threaten** is followed by a 'to'-infinitive (3) or 'that'- clause or by a noun group), you mention the speaker but not the hearer. In a few cases - e.g. in an 'as'-clause functioning as a reporting adjunct (4) - you can avoid mentioning the speaker by using a passive; but the hearer is still not mentioned in these cases, and the subject of the verb is not explicitly mentioned.